Tidal Havens of the Wash and Humber

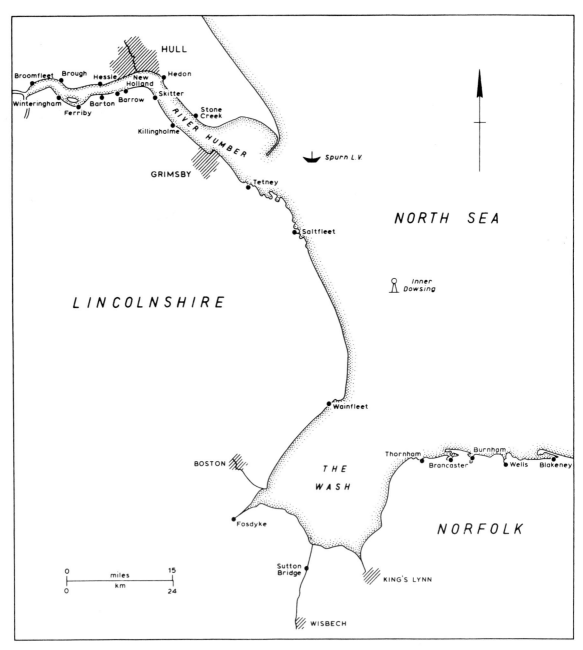

Frontispiece. THE CRUISING GROUND

The Tidal Havens of the Wash and Humber

Henry Irving

Imray Laurie Norie & Wilson
St Ives Cambridgeshire England

Published by
Imray, Laurie, Norie & Wilson Ltd
Wych House, St Ives, Huntingdon, Cambridgeshire PE17 4BT, England

First published 1976
3rd edition revised and reset 1983
4th edition 1991

© Henry Irving 1991

British Library Cataloguing in Publication Data

Irving, Henry
The Tidal Havens of the Wash and Humber.
4th ed.
I. Title
623.89′2294283

ISBN 0 85288 159 2

CAUTION
While every effort has been taken to ensure accuracy, neither the Publishers nor the Author will hold themselves responsible for errors, omissions or alterations in this publication. They will at all times be grateful to receive information which tends to the improvement of the work.

Printed by Tabro Litho, Ramsey Forty-Foot, Huntingdon, Cambridgeshire

Contents

Wells Quay

Prefaces

TO THE FIRST EDITION – 1976

There are not many sections of the British coastline for which a small boat pilot is not available. It is surprising, therefore, that there is not one for the North East coast from Bridlington to Orfordness. It is a long stretch of coast, beautiful in parts, desolate in others, but with no great concentration of industry or large urban areas to lessen its attractiveness as a holiday area. Beaches abound, the sunshine record is good, charming little resorts cater for a wide range of holidaymakers, yet the approaching yachtsman could be forgiven for thinking he is on the very edge of hell, so empty are the waters and so sparse the information. The southern yachtsman venturing north out of the area so beautifully described in Jack Coote's *East Coast Rivers* might probably contemplate a visit to Southwold, Lowestoft and Yarmouth without tremble, for they are conspicuous and simple harbours, and are well covered for boats of all sizes by the Admiralty charts and pilot. Doubts are raised, however, when it is suggested that a cruise be extended north of Yarmouth; there is no familiarity with the place. The northern mariner, on the other hand, is a creature of the rocks, accustomed to his cliffs and conspicuous landmarks; harbours are holes in the rocks or ramparts built out of them; water that is not deep is unsafe. To venture south of Bridlington, south of the stretch of coast described in the Royal Northumberland Yacht Club's *Sailing Directions*, means leaving the cliffs and gulls, the lighthouses and the fortress harbours and exposing one's self, crew and boat to a horrid brown land of swirling tides and shifting sands. As a consequence, the tidal havens of the Wash and Humber are left untouched and undeveloped – a refuge for the yachtsman who likes solitude with adventure and a perfect paradise for the man who likes to contemplate things as they were.

True, there are difficulties, but there are difficulties to the north and to the south when conditions get bad. True, the havens are small, but there are lots of them, and a large section of the boating world must surely subscribe to the opinion that small is beautiful. There are tides and overfalls, sandbanks and eddies, but the area has no monopoly on any of these features, so that a yachtsman who feels confident enough in his seamanship to cruise in strange waters at all can without fear contemplate the Wash and Humber. There is one drawback – the lack of a pilot. Fishing vessels and local yachts sail happily in and out of most of the two dozen or so havens that feature in this publication. There is an immense fund of local knowledge to be tapped. There has never, however, been an attempt to co-ordinate this information into any kind of cohesive whole so that this attractive area, steeped in maritime tradition, can feature in a cruising yachtsman's calculations. This pilot is intended to plug the gap.

I am co-owner of *Venture*, the last of the Paull sailing shrimpers. Sailing fishing vessels reached the apogee of their development at Hull and Grimsby in the early part of this century, yet there is almost nothing left to remind us of this part of our great maritime heritage. The last of the big sailing trawlers have been sold away to Scandinavia, where enthusiasts abound, or to the Faroes, where they are worked as motor fishing vessels until they fall apart. The small trawlers, the Paull and Boston shrimpers, are still to be found as work boats in Lynn, Fosdyke, Boston or Grimsby, but they have never attracted the traditionalists attention commanded in recent years by the Colchester oyster smacks and other similar vessels of the Thames estuary. Only *Venture* remains, and it seems appropriate that I should use her capabilities, her draught and her experience as a yardstick for the compilation of this pilot. There are more than sentimental reasons for this. A draught of 5 feet is more than most modern cruising boats possess. Knowledge that *Venture* has entered all the havens discussed in this pilot should, therefore, be some guarantee of feasibility to the visitor. Approaches, entries and mooring information are given with reference to her capability and manoeuvrability which, by the standards of most modern craft leave a bit to be desired. Most visitors to this cruising ground will have more time, tide and water to play with than is indicated herein. I have not attempted to give separate sets of information for craft of different dimensions; the task would have been too onerous, and there is no problem in this field which cannot be solved by an informed 5 minutes of head work with the local chart. So this is *Venture's* pilot. Without the inspiration she has given me I would never have come to know and love these waters.

But there is more to the project than the old black boat, however strong and beautiful she may be. Without the skill, endurance, enthusiasm and good humour of old *Venture* hands over the years, the pilot would have remained a pipe dream. It is with more than the usual author's sincerity, therefore, that I dedicate this little book to my sailing friends; to *Venture's* co-owner, Dave Snutch, without whose infectious enthusiasm and willingly proferred finance nothing would ever happen; to my oldest friend and sailing mate, Dave Nisbet, whose reserves of strength, courage, incompetence and humour have carried the pair of us over the brink of disaster and back again; to Eric Hammond, Mike Palframan, Alan Dennett, Dick Farrar, John Courtney, Bill Gowland, Barry Speakman, Keith Smithson and Vanessa Stirum, whose patience and skill in putting together things that I have knocked apart go beyond the limits of human imagination.

TO THE THIRD EDITION – 1983

When I wrote the preface to the first edition, in 1976, I was aware that the cruising ground would change. Years of pottering around the havens had shown me the speed and extent of movement of both sand and mud in almost all the places described. I was not surprised, therefore, that a second edition was necessary in 1980 and a third by 1983. What surprised me rather more, however, was the amount of change ashore. The places still look basically the same; there remain dozens of helpful friends and acquaintances scattered around the cruising ground and there has been no sudden upsurge of maritime activity necessitating new marinas and other accoutrements of more crowded coasts. Yet almost everywhere, something has happened which merits mention: a jetty collapses; a pub changes hands and the beer deteriorates; a yacht club builds a new club house with showers – all matters of no great concern to the nation's yachting fraternity but of critical significance to a harassed skipper struggling into a haven in a rainstorm at seven o'clock at night with hungry, crying children aboard.

Other things have happened, too. *Venture* was destroyed at her moorings in Hull by a gale in 1980 but her mantel as representative of traditional sail in the area was picked up and cut in half, one to be donned by the restorers of *Freda and Nora*, a fifty foot Boston smack, and the other by myself in bringing back to Hull from the Faroes, the *William McCann*, a big sailing trawler built in Hull ninety nine years ago. But such craft, big, strong and noble as they are, are not craft for the cruising ground here described. The necessity for limiting draught to 5 feet spurred me on to restore *Venture* in order to re-explore the ground and revise the pilot. In this delightful task I was ably assisted by some old friends and some newer ones, to whom I dedicate this edition – Dave Nisbet, Barry Speakman, Gordon and Rosie Winterton, Alan Dennett, John Kelly, Peter Tomlinson, Ian Martin and Claudia Kirk. Without help of this kind, physical, social and psychological, these tasks would be dull and, for me at least, impossible.

TO THE FOURTH EDITION

Despite the passage of time since the third edition there has been surprisingly little alteration in the basic configuration of the havens. As I write this preface the whole world is in turmoil, and it is a comfort, albeit small, to reflect that in this small corner at least there is an element of continuity. The biggest changes have been man made and, appropriately enough, have occurred in the two large ports covered by the pilot. When the third edition was written change was in sight, but it was shamefully true that Hull and Grimsby did not offer boating facilities to match their distinguished maritime histories. Now Grimsby sports two useful marinas and Hull's splendid facility has become the showpiece of the east coast.

A continuity is also evident in the human back cloth to the cruising grounds. Pressure from the publisher for a speedy revision caused me to turn to friends who still live on the spot, engaged in maritime activity in both a professional and an amateur capacity, and keeping a watchful eye on important changes. I dedicate this edition, therefore, to those among my Wash and Humber friends who have helped me revise the pilot – in particular to Tony Fulford, David Garside, Captain Franklin, Paul Willis, Paul Cooper, Polly Drewry and John Biglin. Without their help it would have been a difficult task these winter months.

Henry Irving
Hull 1991

SKETCH CHART CONVENTIONS

With the exception of two or three of the Fen river harbours, where a sketch would add little to the text, each of the havens described in this pilot is accompanied by one or two sketch maps, designed to assist the user in picking out features which are useful in negotiating entry. These sketches are not substitutes for charts. It is assumed that visitors unfamiliar with the cruising ground will be in possession of up-to-date editions of the appropriate large scale Admiralty charts of the Wash and Humber. For hinterland features, there is no substitute for the various Ordnance Survey maps which cover the area. The sketches simply attempt to combine features of both at an appropriate scale, to suppress features considered unimportant to the processes of approach, entry and mooring, and to highlight those that are considered important.

Buoys, floats and light vessels with their nomenclature for shape, colour, sound and light, are represented in the mode of the Admiralty charts. Beacons and light towers, where they stand as isolated and conspicuous features, are depicted as two-legged tapering structures, rather than as stars, in the interest of chart reading clarity. Lights on jetties and piers are shown as circles with the appropriate labelling. Posts and withies, which feature prominently as navigational aids in many of the havens, are shown as single vertical lines, carrying a top mark when this is the case, and colour labelled in the usual fashion.

Two contours have been shown, though they do not appear on all the sketch charts, for in some cases there is no water in the vicinity of the haven at low tide. Low water ordinary spring tides (LWOST) is the first of the contours. This is a conventional and useful line, for not only does it give an instant impression of the critical underwater relief, but it affords an opportunity to indicate the nature of the bottom, whether rock, shingle, sand, mud or salting. The second selected contour is the fathom line (approx. 1.8m) at low water springs, chosen on the grounds that a skipper requiring a low water anchorage to await the tide into a haven will be able at a glance to know how close to the drying ground he can safely go and to know where he can seek shelter behind banks. Perhaps the most useful contour of all would have been the fathom line at high water neaps. This would show all the places that can be safely navigated by a boat drawing 5 feet (1.5m) on any high water. Some of the Humber havens were indeed surveyed with the aim in mind of providing this contour; for this interesting if muddy exercise I am indebted to my friend John Pethick, whose expertise in the natural history of marsh and dunes comes second only to his extraordinary ability to walk in mud which comes up to his navel. We quickly came to the conclusion that the provision of this contour was probably beyond the capabilities of the Hydrographer to the Navy, let alone the resources behind this pilot, so the attempt was abandoned. Instead, I have adopted the convention of depicting the recommended route into a haven by a thick line of dashes which follows the deepest water.

Features on land are selectively taken from the topographical maps. Not all features are shown, but with charts of such a large scale, most land features have a utility, either as conspicuous markers to assist approaches or as useful guides to land based activities. Roads, ditches, bridges, trees and buildings are, therefore, in nearly all cases fully represented, and if any feature has an obvious utility such as a shop, railway station or public house, it is clearly labelled.

Despite the rapidity of change in these hasty times, the land features are relatively stable and enduring. Only in places like Hull and Grimsby does the demolition hammer cause significant change. Elsewhere, in the backwaters of Holderness, Lincolnshire and Norfolk, little alters from one year to the next. Unfortunately, the same cannot be said for the sands which lace this cruising ground. The Norfolk harbours are always on the move; the approaches to Lynn and Wisbech, despite substantial training efforts, have zones of instability; the upper Humber is so volatile that the Associated British Ports Authority deems it necessary to conduct a bi-monthly survey and produce a chart each time; the slightest obstruction in the Humber havens causes violent swings in the sinuosities of the deep water channels. Perhaps only a fool would attempt to write a pilot for such a restless territory. Yet it is a good place. It merits a lot of attention.

RECOMMENDED CHARTS OF THE CRUISING GROUND

Admiralty
  1190 Flamborough Head to Blakeney Point
 ★ 108 Approaches to the Wash
 ★ 107 Approaches to the Humber
 ★ 109 Entrance to the Humber
  1200 The Wash ports
  1188 River Humber: Spurn Head to Immingham Dock
  3497 River Humber: Immingham Dock to Barton Haven

Associated British Ports
★ River Humber: Spurn Head to Barton Haven
★ River Humber: Barton Haven to Burton Stather
ABP (Humber) Port House, Corporation Road, Hull HU9 5PQ ☎ 0482 27171

Imray, Laurie, Norie & Wilson
  Y9 The Wash
  C28 East Coast. Harwich to Wells
  C29 East Coast of England, Orfordness to Whitby

★ considered essential

Blakeney Harbour

In common with a number of havens described in this cruising ground, Blakeney's fortunes have been in decline since the Middle Ages. The majesty of Blakeney church on the high ground overlooking the harbour stands testimony to the former prosperity of this spot where wealthy Norfolk earth runs down to the sea. Wool export gave way to grain and other agricultural produce, but as late as the eighteenth century Blakeney could still boast a substantial coasting trade. Sailing vessels plied regularly from the quays of Cley and Blakeney to Lynn, Hull, Newcastle and London. There is still a vestigial whiff of the sea about Blakeney, but it is represented by dinghies and shoal draught craft in the main, which, although giving a picturesque air to the scene, do not seem to send the pulse of Norfolk out into the North Sea in the way of yesteryear. Blakeney Harbour is now an area for quiet recreation, a functional backdrop to the National Trust Nature Reserve of Blakeney Point, and the only signs of commerce are the regular summer plying of the ferries from Blakeney and Morston to the Point.

To the cruising yachtsman from the south, however, Blakeney is the first haven north of Yarmouth. This is not merely a psychologically strategic position after more than forty miles of haven-less coast; it can very often happen that a vessel aiming for the more substantial harbour of Wells falls late on the tide – too late for Wells but not too late for Blakeney. In such circumstances, and given the right conditions – no stiff northerly component in the weather and plenty of daylight – the visitor will find in Blakeney a safe and attractive haven with a wide variety of beautiful things to investigate.

BLAKENEY HARBOUR

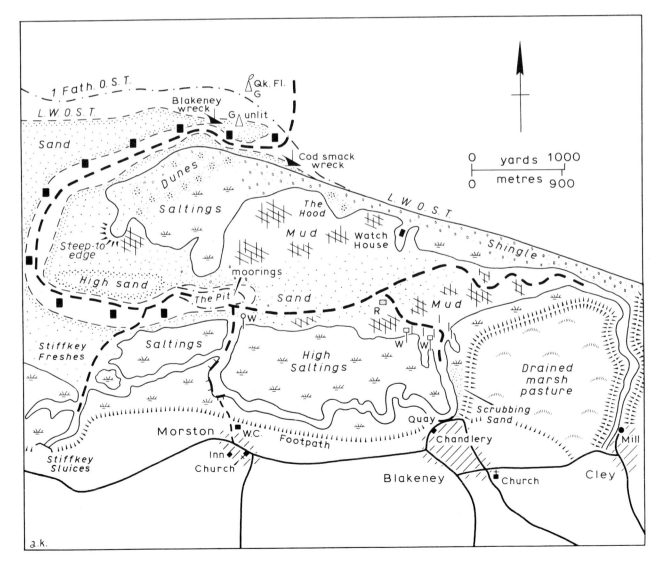

APPROACHES
(See Admiralty
chart no. 108, or
Imray C28)

From the south east, the approaches to Blakeney are extremely simple. The boulder clay cliffs of Cromer and Sheringham give way at Weybourne to the high, steep shingle bank that ends in Blakeney Point. The coast presents no offlying shoals or other dangers, save the occasional crab pot, so the stranger is best advised to sail close inshore with an Ordnance Survey map in his hand so that he can the more easily identify farms and mills as he passes. In anything like reasonable visibility, the tower of Blakeney church will be perceived on the hill one mile to the south, and the first of the entrance markers will be seen some two miles further to the west, just at the point where the dunes bend away to the south west. A quarter of a mile south east of the first buoy is the wreck of a cod smack which poses a danger up to half flood. The mariner is advised to leave at least two hundred yards of water between his vessel and the dunes at this point.

From the north and west the approaches, though free of danger, are less clear cut. Once again, Blakeney church is the most useful general landmark, but the problem lies in spotting the end of the dunes at the point. If the sun is glinting on the sand it is reasonably obvious, but in dull weather care must be taken to spot the wreck buoy before making too close an approach.

A fishing boat disaster in the early 1980s led to the establishment, one cable north of the wreck buoy, of a lit green conical buoy to facilitate night approaches. One is led to doubt the wisdom of such encouragement, however, for none of the other buoys are lit nor do they have radar reflectors. The visitor is strongly advised to regard it as an approaches indicator and to await daylight before attempting entry.

ENTRY

The Blakeney Boatmen's Association maintains a superb set of black can starboard hand markers numbered from 1 to 10. At the time of writing, the channel follows the line of the point, passing south and east of Blakeney Wreck which constitutes a hazard even at HWS. Vessels approaching from the west must leave the wreck buoy to starboard before aiming to round buoy No. 1. It should be remembered, when making this approach, that the tide sets towards the east from two hours before HW, and its strength on springs is sufficient to be a factor of considerable importance in judging any manoeuvre under sail.

For a vessel drawing 5 feet (1·5m), it is possible to enter Blakeney Harbour 2 hours before and up to 2½ hours after spring and mean tides, but on the neaps it is advisable to enter only 1½ hours either side. It is also worth noting that a strong south easterly keeps the water out of the harbour, so in such circumstances it is advisable to wait longer. Both flood and ebb run very strongly around the point, so unless a vessel is equipped with a powerful engine it is worthwhile arranging it so that arrival and departure are made with a favourable tide.

*Blakeney Quay at
low water*

MOORINGS

The handiest and most obvious place to moor in Blakeney Harbour is The Pit, a lagoon of water just in the shelter of the point, where deep water exists at all states of the tide due to its being ponded back by the bar. Unfortunately the area of The Pit is reducing, and it is becoming increasingly congested with permanent moorings. Unless the visitor can find a vacated mooring buoy to occupy he is best advised to proceed up the harbour two or three hundred yards and anchor. Here, all but the shoalest draught vessels will take the ground at low water but there will not be nearly so much risk of coming foul of ground gear. The anchorage is off the entrance to Morston Creek, up which it is possible to row a dinghy for 6 hours or so on each tide to gain access to land facilities. This creek is made conspicuous by the presence, on its eastern marsh side, of an 8 knot speed restriction post which must be left a boat's length to port when entering the creek.

For the visitor who is interested in further penetration into the complex of Blakeney Harbour there are four places which offer possibilities, but neap tides do not provide enough water for any vessel to perform such manoeuvres. For a vessel drawing 5 feet (1·5m), these exercises are only possible on springs. Stiffkey Sluices offers very little except some rather fine sheltered creek berths in which a visitor could lie peacefully for some time, or even safely leave his boat there. From the last conical buoy, No. 10, make south east across the mussel beds taking care to ensure enough draught to avoid touching the mussels. Even the slightest touch can cause tidal scour which might destroy someone's livelihood. A withied channel winds its way into the marsh known as Stiffkey Freshes, and just before the sluices are reached, several steep sided creeks offer mooring possibilities. The marsh is firm, and easy access can be had to the main road.

Morston Creek is the deepest and most substantial of the harbour havens, but it is to some extent monopolised by the ferry operators who take parties of visitors out to Blakeney Point. The landing stages which they have constructed for this purpose provide a useful guide as to which is the deepest side of the creek at any particular place, though in the main the channel is helpfully central. There is no objection to the visiting yachtsman using any of these stages as a temporary mooring, but any interference with the manoeuvres of the ferries will be met with aggression.

The old port of Blakeney has a charming, if rather congested, quay, but it is difficult to imagine that coastal sailing vessels once used it. Neap tides scarcely make at the quay, and even at springs a vessel drawing 5 feet (1·5m) must be prepared to bump occasionally as it feels its way up the tortuous channel. There are withies and small buoys here and there, but several of the withies are not long enough to avoid being covered by a tide that is high enough to facilitate passage. It is advisable that the visitor moors first in The Pit and makes his own low water reconnaissance of the route up to Blakeney Quay. To the east of the quay, by the bend of the channel, there is a very useful patch of hard, sloping sand which is one of the handiest spots for scrubbing off in the whole cruising ground.

An even more tortuous journey awaits the mariner who would fain investigate the other ancient port of Cley. From a point about half a mile east of the entrance to Morston Creek the Cley Channel snakes away to the east past the Watch House, unmarked save for a sporadic buoy or withy. It eventually leads between high banks and bends southwards to the old village of Cley, but half a mile short of the mill the channel becomes so narrow that a vessel of more than 15 feet (4·5m) length will have difficulty in turning. It is probably advisable to regard Cley as an interesting objective for a dinghy trip rather than as a destination for a cruising vessel.

FACILITIES

At Morston there are very few facilities. Lavatories on the dinghy park and a rather quaint pub will be enough to satisfy immediate requirements, but the yachtsman in search of more specialist services will have to press on to Blakeney (E.C. Wed.) Here, the range of shops is considerable – supermarket, baker, post office and the inevitable abundance of trinketry. Particularly useful from the yachtsman's standpoint is the presence of two good chandleries, one of which stocks Calor gas. Being a charming, flint-built village, Blakeney is a popular tourist spot and boasts three residential hotels, a pub and two or three restaurants.

Cley is equally charming, and sports a butcher, a general store, a smoked fish shop, a delicatessen, a garage, a pub and two residential hotels, so that its facilities nicely compensate for any deficiencies in nearby Blakeney. Perhaps the most conspicuous feature of Cley is its beautiful windmill, extremely well preserved. Whether the visit is by road or by the tortuous Cley channel, this beautiful mill is a worthwhile objective.

Wells

The cruising yachtsman who has not sailed into Wells is to be pitied and envied at the same time – pitied for having been hitherto deprived of a real aesthetic experience, envied because such an experience lies ahead. In calm weather, the sheer beauty of rounding the pine wood corner by the coastguard hut, and seeing the little town with its pantiles glinting in the sun, will fill the heart of the hardiest, hairiest and most Philistine of mariners. In sterner weather there can be nothing more productive of adrenalin than passing through the curling white water of the bar and reaching the sanctuary of the harbour behind the east side sand. In heavy weather, especially if there is even a suspicion of north in the wind, there is no future in such manoeuvres, but the soul can still be stirred by gazing out of the windows of the Golden Fleece, by looking at the distant, roaring white surf, and by reflecting that nothing lies between there and the North Pole.

WELLS HARBOUR

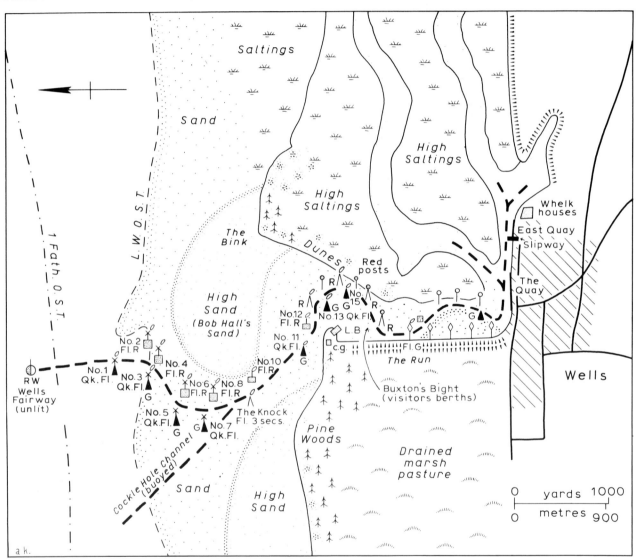

APPROACHES
(See Admiralty chart no. 108, or Imray, Y9, C28)

The north Norfolk coast, in good visibility and quiet weather, is a beautiful, hospitable and varied one, unlike that of Lincolnshire across the Wash. Whether the mariner is approaching from the buoys of the main coastal shipping lane, such as Blakeney Overfalls or SE Docking, or from the Wash buoys such as Burnham Flats or Woolpack, he will have no difficulty in laying and holding a course for the Fairway buoy. The water, though quite shoal in parts, presents few hazards and the tides are not powerful. On becoming familiar with the dunes, sand hills and conspicuous churches of the Norfolk coast, the mariner will have even less difficulty, for he will be able to home in on Wells without much of a thought. One useful homing guide is the long plantation of Holkham Meals. Wells lies immediately at the eastern end of this plantation.

At night, or in fog, it must be one of the most inhospitable coasts in England. Tucked safely away behind the sand hills and marshes, the towns and villages offer no light or sound to guide a navigator. Trinity House has not considered it worthwhile, despite the regular use of the harbour by coasting vessels, to light up the buoys in the offing. When to this uncertainty is added a touch of northerly weather, and the waves begin to break off in the shoaling water, then the skipper who has no familiarity with Wells is strongly advised to stand off and either make for another part of the coast or wait until conditions permit an approach. If the weather is worsening, these may both seem appalling alternatives, but the necessary resolve must be found, for the dangers of an ill-conceived entry into Wells are far more appalling.

ENTRY

Wells may be entered by craft drawing 5 feet (1·5m) on the neapest of tides, but on such occasions the skipper of a vessel this size can only allow himself an hour either side of high. On spring tides, there is more scope. Coasters drawing 10 feet (3·0 metres) use the harbour regularly, so a 5 feet (1·5m) draught boat can usually reckon on entry 2 hours before high water and up to 2 hours after. The entrance channel across the bar and into the harbour is subject to change, but it has a system of buoyage which is relatively stable, relatively standard in form and which is kept lit with as much diligence as can be expected of a harbour authority with a very limited budget.

From the Fairway, the large red No. 2 buoy on the bar itself will be visible in most conditions. It is advisable to make good a course for this until the smaller buoys of the channel become visible, after which it is better to keep towards the starboard side, especially if the wind is westerly, because from 2 hours before HW there is a considerable east-going tidal stream across the harbour entrance. Should a vessel go aground on the east side, (the Bob Hall Sand), then it is extremely unlikely to easily come off again; it will simply be pushed higher up the sand by wind and tide, following the example, presumably, of the unfortunate but unknown Bob Hall. An alternative channel across the bar, known as the Cockle Hole, is a sporadic feature which can permit a more westerly approach to the Knock buoy, as indicated on the sketch chart. When it is deemed to be usefully deep, the harbour authority maintains buoyage.

From the starboard buoy labelled the Knock, the harbour channel bends away towards the south east, and the presence of the Bob Hall sand to seaward renders the remainder of the run in to Wells safe for life and boat if not entirely free from hazard or potential embarrassment. The wide sweep to the eastward opposite the lifeboat shed must be made with the beacons and posts quite close on the port hand for the channel is extremely narrow. Nor does the final southward section down The Run any longer afford an opportunity for much relaxation, for the sand has built out from the western embankment, necessitating a sweep to the east close to the marsh edge.

Wells

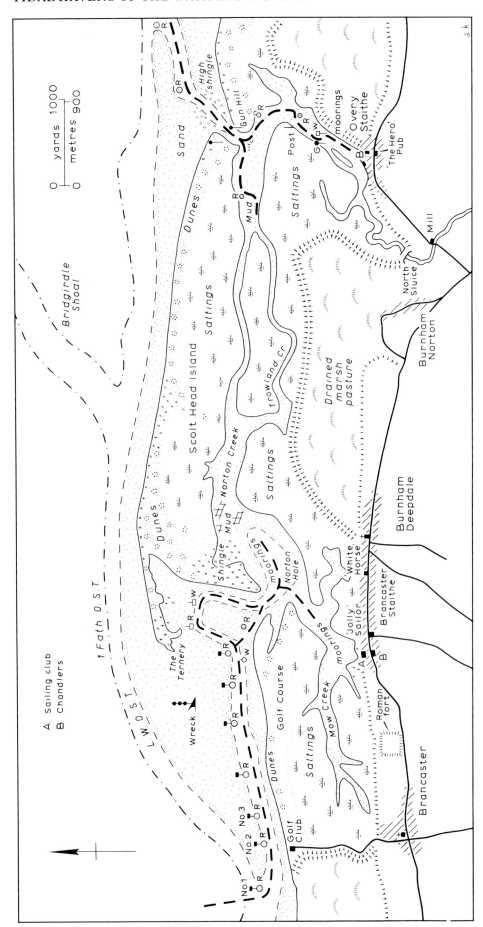

BURNHAM OVERY AND BRANCASTER

MOORINGS   The quay at Wells runs E–W and provides an excellent stopping place until inquiry can be made of the harbour master (☎ (0328) 711646; VHF Ch 16, 12, 37) as to where to moor. When the height of the tide (to the Hull datum) is less than 7·6m, no coasters use the quay and it is likely that a quay berth will be allocated. When the tide is higher than this, the quay is usually busy with coasters and it is not permitted to leave boats un-attended there as it may be necessary to move them around. At such times a berth will usually be allocated at Buxton's Bight, near the lifeboat station. Here some visitor's moorings are laid out in a sheltered area which dries out on flat sand and gives easy shore access to good caravan site facilities.

FACILITIES   Wells is a small town, of some three thousand inhabitants, but it has the bustle, dignity and facilities of a much larger place. Granted it has quietened down from the days when its quay was filled with vessels all the time and its thirty-two taverns reverberated with nautical swagger. Yet the visiting yachtsman still stands to be impressed. Its shops and services are complete as far as day to day cruising needs are concerned. Its eight remaining taverns are lively and friendly. Its elegant town houses will delight the eye of the eighteenth century enthusiast. But at the end of the day it is the people who are the essence of Wells. A considerable proportion of its population are still connected with the sea, in a full time or a part time capacity, and there remains a passionate interest in the quay, the harbour and the boats therein. The visitor can be assured of as much help, advice and friendly conversation as he needs, whilst Standard House Chandlery on the quayside will almost certainly supply those practical requirements that can't be met by conversation alone. (☎ Fakenham (0328) 710593). Fuel is available at Osprey Marine, and a slipway is available on the East Quay with a capacity for vessels up to 45 feet long and up to 25-tons displacement.

Burnham Overy Harbour

Horatio Nelson was born in the parsonage at Burnham Thorpe. It is understandable that local people should take a pride in their illustrious product, but to judge from the Nelsonian bric-a-brac in the shops and pubs of Overy Staithe one would think that The Hero spent his youth breathing the salt air from the top of Gun Hill and cutting his sailing teeth in the treacherous white water of Burnham Harbour mouth. In fact, there is no evidence that young Horatio paid much attention at all to the sea in his childhood. He was sent, from a tender age, to schools in Norwich and North Walsham, and it came as something of a surprise to him when his father decided to send him to sea as a midshipman on his uncle's man o'war. Nelson's first feel of underfoot planking was at Chatham. If it had been at Burnham Overy, he may have had second thoughts.

APPROACHES,
ENTRY
and MOORINGS

Burnham Harbour is very conspicuous from seaward. Indeed, it is perhaps the most identifiable feature on this stretch of the Norfolk coast. The gap in the dunes between Scolt Head Island and the mainland, marked by conspicuous beacons on either side, is unique enough to be almost unmistakable, but the additional feature of Gun Hill, a sand dune situated some hundred yards east of the gap, gives a seal of certainty to the identification process. Having said this, there is little else that can be said to encourage the visiting yachtsman to visit Overy Staithe, charming though it may be. The sand bar outside the harbour moves so frequently that even the local boatmen have difficulty in keeping up to date with their leading features. There is no offlying shelter and even moderate weather from anywhere in the north causes murderous breaking swell which is intensified by the fierce ebb which runs out of the harbour mouth. Once in, there are marker buoys which indicate to the initiated the key turns in the deep water routes into Norton Creek or up to Overy Staithe, but they are so sporadic that the visitor would be lucky indeed to negotiate the channels without prior knowledge or local guidance. Unlike Blakeney and Brancaster, there is no pool where a boat may lie afloat, nor is there a quay, as at Blakeney and Wells, against which to lie.

If, however, the visiting yachtsman has a vessel which can happily take the sand, and if he has a tide to spare for preliminary investigation, then Overy is by no means outside the scope of his cruising itinerary. A vessel drawing 5 feet (1·5m) may enter two hours either side of HWS, depending on the degree of swell, but at neap tides, a high water entry is recommended. The mooring positions of the resident craft will give some indication of the best places to lie, though care must be taken to anchor so as to give swinging room. A

Overy Staithe

keel boat can remain upright by leaning on the steep marsh edge immediately opposite the old staithe. On neap tides, the staithe itself provides a similar facility for shoaler draught keel boats, but at springs it covers and there is such a tidal run that mooring would be difficult. It is possible for a boat drawing 5 feet (1·5m) to make the inshore passage along Norton Creek from Overy to Brancaster or vice versa, but it is essential to have local guidance, for the deep water channel is very tortuous, especially at the Overy end. The tide must be bank full for a vessel of this draught to undertake the passage. Lower than this, there is not enough water; a marsh tide, on the other hand, makes difficult the identification of the sides of the creek.

FACILITIES

Overy Staithe is a beautiful little spot. The subtle mixture of brick and flint in the cottages gives a mellowness to the place that makes a pleasing change from the aggressive appearance of the all-flint villages. The local pub, The Hero, is an unexceptional establishment, but a two mile walk to Burnham Thorpe will be rewarding to connoisseurs of beer and naval history alike, for Les Winter at the Nelson is a mine of Nelsonian information and a fount of excellent Greene King beer. There are few other facilities in this charming village, but the active dinghy sailing community supports an excellent chandlery, the owner of which, Peter Beck, (☎ (0328) 73348) is himself a keen sailing enthusiast and the most reliable authority on the state of navigation of the haven. In good weather, a pilgrimage to Nelson's birthplace can add a lot to the cruising experience.

Brancaster Harbour

In the third century AD, the Romans, concerned about the crumbling periphery of their empire, established a series of Saxon shore forts on the East coast of England to defend the land against the Germanic invaders. The north Norfolk coast was protected by a series of watch towers and forts, but the most important of all was that at Brancaster, where a cavalry troop was stationed. It is not clear from historical evidence whether the Romans made much use of such harbour facilities as nature provided, but it does seem likely, even at that time, that an offlying sand spit gave shelter from the sea in much the same way as it does now. As centuries passed, however, the spit extended to the east and the haven behind it was colonized with salt marsh so that the creeks became too shallow and narrow to be of even local commercial importance. The local fishermen of the area founded a new settlement, Brancaster Staithe, some two miles to the east of Brancaster, where a deeper and wider creek flowed right up to the hard shingle of the rising shore. The formation, during medieval times, of the offshore bar now known as Scolt Head, gave additional protection to the harbour, supporting a flourishing whelk industry second only to Wells in the whole of Britain.

APPROACHES

Although the normal strictures about fog, darkness and heavy northerly weather hold true for Brancaster as for all the other harbours of north Norfolk, it is probably the least severe of them all. The curving spits at the west end of Scolt Head and the drying sand which juts beyond them at all but the highest of tides afford a protection to Brancaster Bay which is denied to all other places along this stretch of coast. In particular, north easterlies are to be feared less here than in the other harbour approaches. An additional advantage is the presence of unusually deep water in Brancaster Roads off Scolt Head, giving an anchorage even for large vessels that is protected from all but the worst of weather by the encircling Bridgirdle Shoal to the north.

In clear weather, Scolt Head provides a conspicuous landmark. Its treeless dunes are significantly higher than the dunes along other sections of the coast, and the fact that it stands so far to seaward enables the mariner to put it in three dimensional relief with the rising ground behind much more quickly than is possible with the other dune ridges. The entrance to Brancaster harbour lies some 2½ miles to the south west of the head itself, and its approximate position can be identified by the prominent buildings of the Royal West Norfolk Golf Club house on the dunes fronting Brancaster village. A conspicuous wreck, marked with a beacon carrying three black balls arranged vertically and visible even at high water, is a further identifying feature lying about half way between Scolt Head and the harbour entrance.

ENTRY

A boat drawing 5 feet (1·5m) can enter the harbour with safety some 2½ hours either side of HWS. At neaps, a safe position may be reached two hours before high water, though shoal ground will be encountered further up the harbour and it may be as late as one hour before high before the mooring positions in Norton Hole can be attained. The ebb tide runs fiercely out of the harbour from half an hour after high water, so it is advisable to time the arrival so as to avoid punching it.

The outer buoyage is clear and conspicuous, though unlit apart from a flashing white light mounted on a pole near the golf club house which serves to orient the nocturnal visitor but is no invitation to entry. At the outer end of the sand bar to the west of Scolt is the first of a series of five or six red spherical buoys with red rectangular topmarks which the harbour authority attempts to maintain as mid channel markers. This first buoy is situated about half a mile to the westward of the golf club house. It is essential that vessels approaching from the east should round this mark, for high water routes across the bar are unmarked and uncertain. An ingoing vessel should pass close to all the buoys until the last of the series is reached. By this time sufficient shelter will be available from Scolt to avoid danger if not discomfort.

The last red buoy of the series can be identified by the presence, close to the south of it, of a large white sailing club marker buoy. From here, the deepest water can be taken by turning towards the north, towards the spit of Scolt known as the Ternery. The local fishermen, who use this route to get their whelks home as early as possible on the tide, attempt to mark the principle bends in the channel by a polyglot series of buoys whose characteristics change as soon as the back is turned. The final southward leg of the Ternery route should be run close to the mainland shingle before turning east towards the Norton Hole moorings.

A more convenient route, and one which has only a foot or so less water than the Ternery channel, leads from the red and white 'twin' buoys directly south east along the steep-to shingle bank of the mainland spit. A faded red spherical buoy gives the direction of the route, which can be maintained right into Norton Hole.

MOORINGS

A vessel drawing 5 feet (1·5m) can lie afloat, though only just afloat, in the deepest part of Norton Hole. The mooring buoys nearest the entrance carry the deepest water, and the visitor can usually find one vacant, especially outside the peak sailing season. It is vastly preferable to borrow a mooring wherever possible, for the fierce ebb tide through the harbour entrance will provide a stern test for even the mightiest ground gear. The creeks dry out, more or less, away from Norton Hole. If solitude is sought, and if the opportunity of exploring the National Trust reserve of Scolt Head is an attraction, then Norton Creek is the one to head for. If, on the other hand the facilities of Brancaster Staithe have more pull, then a turn to starboard up Mow Creek will be more convenient. There are many boats at moorings and at anchor in Mow Creek, and they all swing to the tide and dry out, so great care must be taken when selecting a spot to anchor. Communication with the harbour master, Mr. M. Nudds (☎ (Brancaster) 210638) may result in the allocation of a temporary mooring or at least advice as to the best anchorage in an area that is festooned with active mussel lays.

FACILITIES

Brancaster Staithe is a straggling village, not nearly so charming as the nucleated villages to the west and east, Brancaster and Burnham Deepdale. Yet it has a number of facilities which will recommend it to the visiting yachtsman. The sailing club, perched on the shingle hard to the east of the whelk houses, has bar, shower and drying facilities. Across the main road is Borthwick's Boatyard, which, although mainly catering for the interests of dinghy sailors, does have a range of chandlery. One hundred yards to the east, on the main road, is the Jolly Sailor, a rather fancy pub with a high quality restaurant attached. The White Horse, half a mile further to the east, provides more down to earth pub facilities, and the scatter of services in between – 2 garages, a general store and a post office – should satisfy the more immediate requirements of the visitor.

Thornham

For a port to flourish in north Norfolk during the late eighteenth and early nineteenth century it needed simply to provide a facility to export grain and to import coal. Thornham, with its own creek-threaded marsh and protective girdle of dunes, provided such a facility, so it flourished. A water colour in the Life Boat inn shows Thornham staithe at the beginning of this century with its grain barn and its coal barn. Now, unfortunately,

THORNHAM
HARBOUR

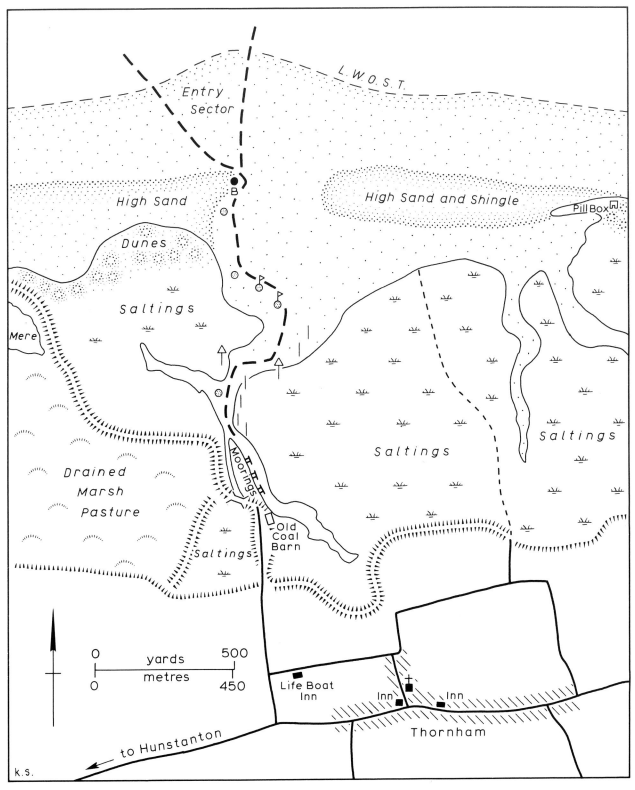

Thornham coal barn and creek

only the coal barn remains, but this tiny flint-built warehouse is a gem of industrial archaeology and it does not stretch the imagination too far to envisage a creek bustling with 'billy boys' and sailing barges. The creek today has lost its bustle but it retains its beauty and aura of the past. For this reason alone it is worth a visit and it presents no serious problems in settled weather.

APPROACHES
(See Admiralty chart no. 108, or Imray Y9)

Thornham is not easy to identify from seaward, for its houses and church lie buried in trees. From the west, a passage through the Bays between the Sunk and the Gore Middle Sands will give a heading on Titchwell church – a feature not always as conspicuous as the Admiralty chart suggests owing to it being extremely slender and surrounded by trees. Three miles east of Hunstanton cliffs and old lighthouse there is a break in the dunes which marks the entrance to Thornham harbour. From the east, the West Norfolk Golf Club, situated at the entrance to Brancaster harbour, is the most conspicuous shore feature; some two miles west of that occurs the break in the dunes, this eastern dune being surmounted by a wartime pill-box.

Thornham Bays provide an admirable low water anchorage for reconnaissance, being protected by the Gore Middle Sand to the north. This covers fairly early on the tide, however, and after covering it is not long before the sea becomes very uncomfortable in any significant wind from the northerly parts. A skipper bent on low water exploration must be prepared to feel around with lead line or echo sounder before selecting an anchorage, for the sand deposits fronting the Thornham creeks are irregular in shape and depth.

ENTRY and MOORINGS

It is not feasible for a vessel drawing 5 feet (1·5m) to visit Thornham on extremely neap tides. The shelter of the creeks is attainable, but the mooring jetties will not carry sufficient water. On mean tides or above, however, there is plenty of water right up to the staithe and 1½ hours either side of high water is a sensible margin to work with. Naturally, shoaler draught vessels and those which can bottom happily will be able to give themselves much more scope. The local fishermen make a sterling attempt to keep the channel marked, though this cannot be relied on and a newcomer is advised to make a low water reconnaissance prior to entry. A black buoy marks the western side of the entrance and is moved as the high sand advances or retreats. Further up the channel at frequent intervals and always indicating the major bends, there are several small buoys of many shapes and colours. These are essentially starboard markers and must be passed extremely close as the channel is not very wide. When the salt marsh is reached, posts on either bank surmounted by triangular topmarks indicate the position of the deepest water, and the final run south to the moorings necessitates giving the east bank, marked by small posts, a reasonably wide berth.

Mooring jetties in the creek are all privately owned, but if one is spare a visitor is welcome to use it. Failing this, a mooring outside a boat of appropriate dimensions is very feasible for the bottom of the creek though fairly hard is flat bottomed and there are no awkward contours which might cause a boat to lie heavily. For this same reason, a berth against the high marsh edge opposite the mooring jetties is also a perfectly acceptable alternative.

FACILITIES

Thornham (E.C. Wed.) is not only picturesque but also a village of some substance. A butcher, baker, post office, two grocers and a garage make revictualling extremely convenient, whilst thirst and desire for conviviality can be quenched at one of its three pubs. The two in the village are part of what was the Watney empire, but the discerning drinker will probably never discover this, for the Life Boat, nearest the staithe, sells a variety of good beer including Tolly's of Ipswich and Greene King of Bury St Edmunds. This is, without doubt, some of the best fare that East Anglia can offer.

King's Lynn

Lynn was one of the great seaports of medieval England. It is perhaps not at all a bad thing, from the standpoint of the visiting yachtsman, that its greatness is a thing of the past. So often, the increase in scale consequent on industrial and commercial progress serves to bury the trappings of the past, and ports are particularly susceptible to such burials. It is not that Lynn has made no modern industrial progress; it is one of East Anglia's growth towns, and its suburbs are littered with light industrial developments which indicate prosperity if they do not enhance beauty. Rather, it is the lack of progress in seaborne commerce which has relieved historic Lynn from the fate which has befallen many of its medieval partners in maritime prosperity. A dock system has been built, but it is relatively small and downstream of the historic core; factories and silos dot the quayside, but they do not intrude severely on to the traditional scene. Pre-industrial Lynn stands surprisingly unscathed. A voyage into this ancient port is a voyage into the very maritime and commercial history of England.

APPROACHES
(See Admiralty
charts nos. 1200,
108 or Imray Y9)

The main route into the Wash, past the Lynn Well to the Roaring Middle light float is straightforward, well charted and well-lit. If bound for Lynn, the incoming skipper is advised to leave the Roaring Middle about 2 miles to starboard and to proceed in a southerly direction until Lynn No. 1 buoy is picked up. The Lynn pilots normally are on station to the north east of No. 1 buoy when a vessel is expected, and so provide an additional identification feature. The buoyage in from this point is clear, frequent and standard. If a vessel is early on the tide, it is advisable to enter Cork Hole and to proceed as far as the No. 5 starboard hand buoy before seeking anchorage. In this way shelter can be obtained from the surrounding sands and there can be guaranteed a more peaceful sojourn than can be had further to seaward. The incoming tide in Cork Hole can attain 2½ knots on springs, so it is advisable to lay out ground gear in which some confidence can be placed.

Lynn waterfront. Purfleet and South Quay

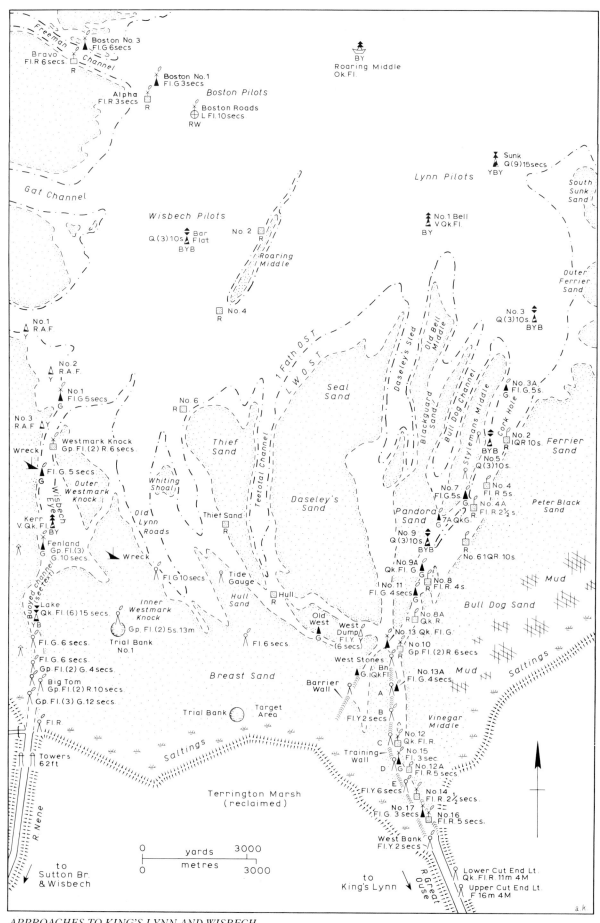

APPROACHES TO KING'S LYNN AND WISBECH

Another approach to Lynn is provided by the Old Lynn Channel, a former main approach which sweeps around the western side of the Roaring Middle and the Thief Sand. It has a residual, sporadic and unlit buoyage system which can serve as a guide to the knowledgeable but siren to the ignorant. In an attempt to prevent the tide from spreading its scouring efforts in more than one direction, a barrier wall was constructed in 1966 to restrict the flow in and out of this channel. To some extent this was successful, for the Old Lynn Channel is not so deep as it used to be; in another sense it failed, for there is a residual scour to the north of the barrier wall which affords an alternative approach to Lynn. It is one often used by local fishing boats but there is no conceivable reason why a yachtsman coming in from the sea would want to choose this channel rather than the main one. It does, however, provide a useful short passage between the Ouse and the Wisbech rivers. If this can be done quickly, across the high water, then there are few problems for the careful navigator. The more leisurely skipper, wishing to use his tides efficiently, might prefer to ebb out of one river, sit out the low water in an anchorage, and enter the

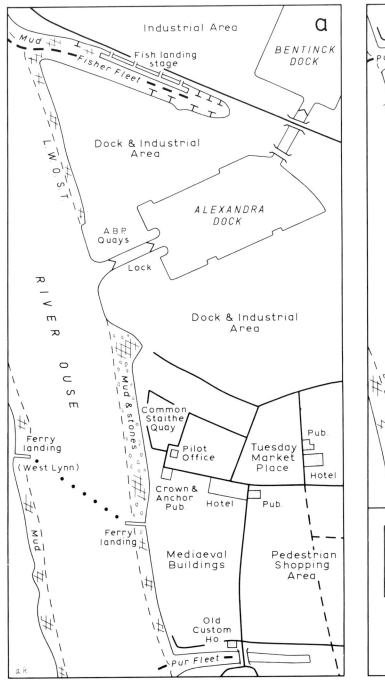

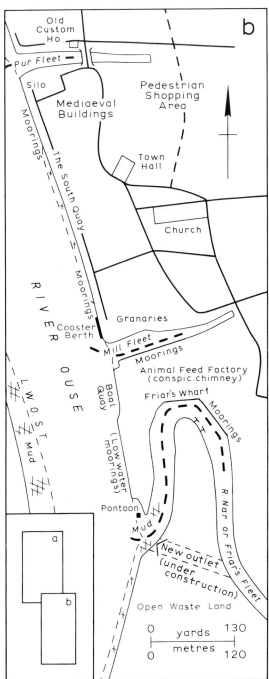

Congestion in Fisher Fleet

other on the flood in the usual way. There is just such an anchorage near the Old West buoy. The tranquillity of this sand-girt spot, together with the abundance of cockles in the vicinity, make this a rewarding experience.

ENTRY

The Ouse outfall silts up in the way of all Wash rivers and only shoal draught vessels can use it over the low water period of neap tides. At low water springs there is not enough water for anything. A craft drawing 5 feet (1·5m) can safely proceed across the shoal to the south of No. 5 buoy four hours either side of high water. On big spring tides, which are often delayed, it is better to wait until 3½ hours before high before attempting entry. A skipper bound for the sea from Lynn on the ebb must have due regard for the mileage involved and the weather when making his judgement as to the length of time it will take to get from Lynn to deep water.

The channel into Lynn from the head of Cork Hole is well marked with standard lit port and starboard marker buoys and presents no difficulty by day or night. The West Stones beacon, a prominent starboard hand light some 3 miles south of No. 7 buoy, marks the end of a training wall built in 1969 to ensure more stability in the Lynn Channel. This wall, marking the west side of the Ouse outfall for the last 3 miles into the river proper, dries 9 feet (2·7m) at low water, but covers well before high. Frequent beacons, some of them lit, prevent this from posing any problems except in thick fog. A similar, but much shorter training wall extends to seaward on the eastern, or Lynn side of the channel for about 1 mile.

MOORINGS

As late as the mid-nineteenth century, Lynn was threaded with waterways known as 'fleets' – tidal sections of numerous streams which drained into the Ouse in and around the town. Drainage has since been rationalised so that the fleets of Lynn now survive only as truncated apologies for their former importance. Some of them still serve as mooring places; others are so silted that they cannot accommodate even the shoalest draught.

The first possibility, on approaching the town, is the Fisher Fleet, a drying tidal creek running inland for about a quarter of a mile. Lynn boasts a considerable number of in-shore fishing boats, both smacks and seiners, and they use the Fisher Fleet to land their catches. There has been constructed a substantial fish quay on the north side of the fleet, but it is rarely possible to find a mooring space there. In fact, such is the congestion and activity in this fleet that it is not recommended as a mooring spot for the visitor unless he is possessed of a vessel of equivalent robustness to a seiner.

A little further upstream lies the entrance to Lynn Docks – two docks owned by Associated British Ports (☎ (0553) 2636) which are given over in the main to the timber, fertilizer and grain trades. They are busy little docks and the authorities discourage pleasure craft from entering unless in an emergency. On spring tides a level is made 2 hours before high water and the gates are closed half an hour after high water. Ingress and egress is normally only permitted on the level water, though when the time of level is more restricted, as is the case on the neapest of tides, some locking is undertaken.

Upstream of the dock entrance is a shelving section of the river bank that is unsuitable for mooring. The round tower of the sixteenth-century pilot house, used by the Lynn pilots to this day, is an attractive and conspicuous feature of this stretch. Beyond this is the Purfleet, a fleet of considerable importance in the Lynn of yore, as is witnessed by the splendid 17th-century custom house at its head. The recent closure of the land drainage outlet in the Purfleet has, however, led to severe silting, and its utility as a mooring for deeper draughted boats is restricted to spring tides. There are, however, plenty of available berths in this historic part of Lynn on the South Quay, upstream of the Purfleet. The quay dries out, except on extremely neap tides, leaving a bottom of fairly hard and gently sloping mud, so that keel boats are advised to make mast rope arrangements.

At the south end of the quay is another fleet, the Mill Fleet, which has moorings along its southern side. This fleet is quite well used by local boatmen, but a mooring can usually be found towards the mouth. Care must be taken on entering the Mill Fleet, for high banks of hard mud project from both corners. A central entry is recommended.

Immediately adjacent to the Mill Fleet, on its southern side, is Boal Quay, a peninsula formed by the hooked mouth of the river Nar. This quay, and indeed the whole of the peninsula, is council-owned, and provides deep water moorings at all states of the tide. The large rise and fall of tide, combined with the fragmented and silt-coated nature of the quay ladders, makes the Boal Quay a less than convenient mooring, but its all-tide qualities make it a noteworthy facility.

Millfleet

The river Nar, or Friar's Fleet, marks the southern edge of the town and provides a number of drying moorings for local boat owners. Some boats lie about half a mile up the Nar, near the main road bridge to South Lynn, but the visitor is not recommended to waste time navigating the tortuous creek as far as that. There are rarely vacant berths and it is a most unhandy and squalid location. On top of this, the water authority are, at the time of writing, in the process of blocking the Nar and creating a sluice outfall into the main stream of the Ouse. When this happens, only the truncated section around Friar's Wharf will remain, and no doubt siltage will occur. For the moment it is used by fishing boats unable to find a berth in the Fisher Fleet, but there are often several vacant berths for visitors. There is really little to tempt the visitor to use fleet berths in Lynn any more, except if contemplating leaving his vessel unattended; the local boatmen, requiring privacy, cheapness and shelter have carved out their own patches in the fleets. For the normal cruising requirements the South Quay and the Boal Quay provide an abundance of adequate berths.

Friar's Wharf, on the
bend of the Nar

A mooring anywhere between Purfleet and the Nar is an extremely convenient one from the point of view of victuals and services. The old medieval core of Lynn is not only attractive to behold, but owing to some complex and imaginative planning remains the essential commercial heart of the town today. A pedestrianised shopping area and an old market square contain most of the kinds of shop that a visitor would ever require. Lynn is as compact and water orientated a service centre as can be found in the whole cruising ground. Being also a rail head, an increasingly rare feature of this part of the country, it is an ideal spot for starting a cruise or changing crew.

Craft with lowering masts or without masts at all, can pass under Lynn road bridge and gain access to the vast network of placid inland waterways that threads the Fens. The cathedral city of Ely, the university city of Cambridge and the delightful market towns of the Ouse valley – St Ives, Huntingdon and St Neots – are extremely worthwhile cruising objectives.

Wisbech

The highway name board on the main road approaches to Wisbech proclaims that it is 'Capital of the Fens'. Certainly, its position deep in the heart of the orchard and strawberry country of the silt fen have ensured the town a solid agricultural prosperity which is very apparent to the visitor. But Wisbech, unlike its neighbour Spalding, has refused to turn its back on the sea. Signposts lead the motorist to the quay by the Nene as though it symbolised the prosperity of the town, and the magnificent terraces of merchant's houses on the river banks above the bridge have to this day an appearance of purpose and enterprise that no insular farmers' houses could ever assume. There are usually far too few commercial vessels to give the quay a sense of bustle, but Wisbech remains firmly a seaport and is the more attractive for it. It is not significantly further inland than the other Wash ports, and its special attractions make it well worth a visit.

A mile to the west of the Roaring Middle sandbank lies Bar Flat buoy, the waiting station of the Wisbech pilots. This buoy is only visible in clear and calm conditions from the Roaring Middle light float, a distance of just over three miles, so great care must be exercised with the helm if visibility is poor. The course from the Roaring Middle to Bar Flat

*Wisbech. Merchant's houses
along the Nene*

(218 degrees True) should be maintained right into the Wisbech channel where the buoyage is clear, frequent and lit. If a vessel is too early on the tide for an entry into the Nene, and a peaceful anchorage is required, the Outer Westmark Knock affords excellent shelter from any inclement wind or sea that may be following in from the north. There is deep water in the channel as far as the Wreck buoy, and soundings in the pool to the south east of this buoy will yield a variety of good places to lie at anchor, though it must be remembered that the spring flood can exceed two knots.

ENTRY   In common with the other Wash rivers the Nene is inaccessible from the sea until 3 hours before high water for craft drawing 5 feet (1·5m), and three hours after high water is the latest safe time for crossing the bar at Fenland buoy. This limitation means that an outward bound vessel is advised to leave Wisbech before high water if it can effectively punch the tide, for the distance, combined with possible delays at Sutton swing bridge, can rapidly eat into those 3 hours. Unless his craft is possessed of a powerful engine or is lucky enough to command a stiff southerly breeze, the outbound mariner is going to be on limits at the Fenland buoy. A more relaxing way of quitting Wisbech, if time is available, is to leave the town sometime on the ebb tide previous to the one planned for sea departure. A mooring can be had for the duration of the flood tide below Sutton bridge or at the Nene Towers.

The channel from the Fenland buoy to the Nene towers is tortuous and variable, and the sinuosities across the bar are marked by a standard buoyage system which upon occasions can resemble a slalom course. The Kerr N cardinal buoy must be left close to port, then in turn No. 1 green to starboard, No. 2 red to port, No. 3 green to starboard and No. 4 red to port before finally leaving the Lake S cardinal to starboard. From here the channel is clearly marked by a series of starboard hand beacons, all showing lights. There is one port hand beacon, Big Tom, about a mile to seaward of the outfall. The river itself, trained between high banks, runs more or less straight in a direction just west of south for some 3½ miles to Sutton swing bridge. This bridge carries the busy A17 trunk road across the Nene, but it has a continuous watch and will open on request at any state of the tide. V.H.F. radio is installed at the bridge, on Ch 16 and 19; if planning from shore, of course, the bridge keeper can be contacted by telephone (Holbeach (0406) 350364). If sound signals are carried on board, the letter B (one long three short) will open the bridge. If none of these aids are appropriate, the time-honoured bellow and wave will no doubt work, but it must be remembered that the tide runs hard and the traffic runs thick and fast. Traffic signals – red, amber and green – indicate the state of play at night. Above the bridge, the Nene continues in a similar direction between high banks for another 7½ miles up to Wisbech fixed bridge, with occasional bank beacons to give night guidance.

Sutton bridge from pilot wharf showing floating pontoon

Vessels passing up and down the Nene will most usually be operating on the upper parts of a tide, and depths in the river will present no problems. Occasionally, however, and especially if a double-stage exit from Wisbech is being executed, it may be convenient and necessary to move on the lower phases of the tide. It is worth noting, therefore, that a boat drawing 5 feet (1·5m) can pass up and down the Nene at low water anywhere between the Towers and the bend that is situated one mile above Sutton Bridge. Between this bend and Wisbech, however, there is insufficient water for this kind of manoeuvre.

MOORINGS

There are several places where mooring is possible in the Nene below Sutton swing bridge. These moorings can only be regarded as temporary but their strategic utility for a downstream passage has already been mentioned. At the foot of the western tower is a substantial jetty with a good ladder which gives the seagoing vessel the very best jumping off point for a northward passage to the Humber. The pilots have been known to object to craft mooring on this jetty, but they can usually be reassured if the stay is only for a tide.

About half a mile below Sutton Bridge, on the west bank just upstream of the new commercial quays, is the site of an old tidal dock which used to be of some commercial importance. The dock has long been infilled, but the piled quays on either side of the former entrance have deep water against them at all but the lowest states of the tide. These quays are used by the handful of fishing smacks which operate out of Sutton Bridge, so care must be taken not to interfere with activity, but a mooring can usually be obtained here.

From Sutton Bridge to Wisbech the banks are shoal and no mooring can be made, but, in any event, there is very little in the flat fen country to tempt the visitor to arrest his progress. Wisbech itself, on the other hand, offers a mileage of quay space that is almost embarrassing in its munificence. It is prudent, however, to consult the harbour master (☎ (0945) 61369) before selecting a permanent mooring spot. The principle commercial quay is on the east bank, extending about a mile downstream from the bridge. Coasting vessels, engaged principally in the grain and fertilizer trade, tie up to various berths along this quay. The safest, and most convenient quay space for pleasure craft is close to the bridge on either bank, where a visitor can either moor outside a barge or make his own quayside arrangements. The rise and fall is considerable, being about 20 feet (6 metres) on spring tides and 11 feet (3.3 metres) on neaps, and the tides run strongly owing to the rather constricted nature of the channel through the town, but the bed of the river is of soft mud and no mooring difficulties will be encountered. Some quay berths have deep water at all states of the tide; others dry out a little, but it would be a thankless task to attempt to specify precisely how much water is available on all parts of the quay. For this, there can be no substitute for immediate local advice. No harbour dues are payable for small craft in the port of Wisbech.

FACILITIES   There are no facilities at the Tower mooring save the possibility of begging water from a farmhouse. The New Inn at Gedney Drove End lies four miles away along fen roads, and most yachtsmen will be reluctant to make such an effort in search of 'vin de pays'. Those who do, however, will find the quality of the welcome and the quality of the Elgood's Bitter second to none. More searching requirements must be sought at Sutton Bridge, a rather unattractive linear settlement straddling the A17 at the point where it crosses the Nene. All the basics for solid and liquid refreshment may be had at Sutton Bridge, but the visitor is strongly advised to make his long Wash journey worthwhile by pressing on for seven miles through the Fen to Wisbech (E.C. Wed, Market day Thurs). Here the full facilities of a prosperous little port and market town can be sampled. In particular the locally-brewed Elgood's beer will serve extremely well that mundane but nonetheless critically important function of slaking the raging maritime thirst.

As with Lynn, Wisbech is not the water's end. It is merely the lowest fixed bridging point. The Nene beyond can take the mastless visitor on through the fen to the Dog in the Doublet Sluice, where he can escape from the tide and journey on, through Peterborough, Oundle, Thrapston, Wellingborough and Northampton into the very heart of England. Such a voyage, however, is beyond the scope of this pilot, and the enthusiast is referred to *Imray's map of the River Nene*. For the mariner, all that is left is the straight and muddy channel to the north, to the sands and to the open sea.

Boston and Fosdyke

A commemorative tablet of stone stands in a field near the Witham, half way between Boston and the sea, testifying to the fact that a large contingent of those who eventually sailed from Plymouth as Pilgrim Fathers hailed from Boston. The naming of the great Massachusetts seaport indicates the nostalgia of this group, and reflects the solid and lengthy maritime tradition of the Lincolnshire port. It always surprises the more discerning and heritage-conscious American visitors, therefore, that Boston remains unsung on the tourist itineraries. Yet, despite this neglect, the magnificent church of St Botolph, more affectionately known to generations of homecoming sailors as the Stump, remains serene and unruffled above its pantiled town and miles of rich fen. Boston's peace and prosperity remain, owing nothing to the ephemeral world of the tourist.

There is certainly nothing wrong with the place, and to the visiting yachtsman Boston offers a great deal. Its approaches are safe and free from problems; its port facilities are reasonably good, and it attracts a mixture of commercial, fishing and pleasure vessels which live in unusual harmony one with the other. Perhaps it is simply the distance from the open sea which deters the visitor. It is indeed a long sail from Lynn Knock to the Boston Stump, and for the mariner who has no interest in penetration then this distance could seem irksome. Yet a voyage through the sands of the Wash is both interesting and exciting in its own right; the town of Boston is an excellent place for a boat-based sojourn; and for those craft with lowering masts, the Grand Sluice offers access to miles of Fenland navigable drains and to the Trent and canal systems beyond. (See Derek Bowskill's *Northeast Waterways*, Imray).

APPROACHES
to the Witham
and the Welland
(See Admiralty
chart no. 1200
and Imray Y9)

There are two approaches to this western corner of the Wash. The passage through the Wainfleet Swatchway and the Boston Deep is described elsewhere, in the Wainfleet section. In good visibility there are no problems with the Boston Deeps; it is simply a question of sailing along a wide and reasonably straight channel from one buoy to the next. At night there are problems, for the buoys are not lit. This passage is not recommended in such circumstances.

By far the best used approach to Boston, and the one used by commercial shipping, is the buoyed and lit Freeman Channel which leads from the Lynn Well, between the Long Sand and the Roger Sand, into the south western section of the Boston Deep. There is deep water here at all states of the tide, so that even quite large commercial vessels can pass through at LWS to find a relatively sheltered anchorage and await the incoming tide before proceeding further.

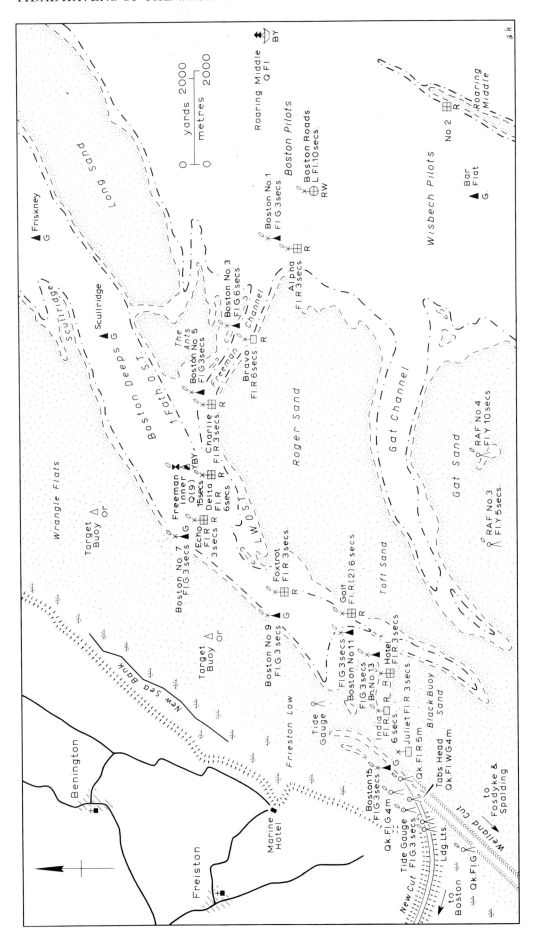

APPROACHES TO BOSTON AND WELLAND

Boston Stump and fish quay

ENTRY
to the Witham
and Welland

Both these Fenland rivers, which converge at Tabs Head Beacon, drain large land areas and both therefore contain substantial, if varying, amounts of water even at low tide. It is not possible, however, to effect an entrance to these rivers at LWS, even with the shoalest draught craft, for there is deposited, just to seaward of their convergence, a considerable amount of silt and sand. Indeed, craft drawing 5 feet (1·5m) or more are advised to wait until 3 hours before high water before attempting to go west of the Upper Sea Head buoy. On a neap tide I have sailed *Venture* down the Witham, around Tabs Head and up the Welland over the low water period, but this is not a manoeuvre which offers much joy, for after two or three miles the bed of the Welland is inevitably encountered, and if anything takes longer to happen than a watched kettle it is a neap flood.

The channels of the Welland and Witham are both embanked, straight and clearly marked with lit beacons, so that by day or night the mariner should have no trouble in making swift and effective progress up whichever one he chooses. The one hazard in these parts is the fog. Not only is the area subject to its normal share of blanket fogs which afflict this part of the North Sea and Fenland, but also the quiet merging of land and water in this corner of the Wash gives rise to a high incidence of thin but perilous inversion fog. It is little comfort to the groping skipper to know that the top of his mast is in clear moonlight. He can only pray that a local fishing boat comes past to guide him in before a coaster appears to mow him down.

MOORINGS
and
FACILITIES
in Boston

The first feature encountered on sailing up the Witham to Boston is the Dock, a small but extremely busy municipally-owned wet dock, engaged principally in the timber, fertilizer and grain trade. The harbour master (☎ (0205) 362328) does not encourage the use of the dock by fishing or pleasure craft, for there is usually severe commercial congestion, but in an emergency or in relatively slack times the visitor can be accommodated within. It is a strict ruling in such circumstances, however, that the craft should be attended at all times in case movement is required. The locks are manned from 2½ hours before HW to 1½ hours after, and unless the tide is a particularly poor one, there is usually a period of level water which makes ingress and egress more simple. The river quay on the upstream side of the dock entrance provides a suitable place to moor provided care is taken not to interfere with the usual berths of the pilot boats, fishing boats and occasional coaster. This mooring causes less problems with drying out than any other in Boston for the mud is extremely soft. The disadvantages of this berth are that it is dirty and noisy from dock activity and that it is at considerable remove from the town facilities. Moreover, it would not be wise to leave a boat unattended here for more than a few hours at a time.

A much safer and more attractive part of Boston in which to moor lies above the railway swing bridge which remains open to river traffic unless the dock railway is being used. Here, numerous substantial jetties line the banks, and although craft will take the mud, a private jetty usually indicates a level and soft bottom which will create no problems. If none of these jetties can be negotiated on a temporary basis, the visitor still has the option of proceeding right up to the new bridge. Here, the fish quay is on the right, and the constant activities of the shrimp smacks preclude a peaceful sojourn, but there are a couple of good private moorings with ladders on the opposite bank near the crab canning factory. There is a considerable fall of tide before a vessel will bottom in the soft mud here, so long scope on the lines is advisable, but this mooring does have the advantage that it can be reached and left easily on half tide.

This mooring position places the visitor deep in the heart of Boston. It is only a short walk to shops, market, taverns, banks and the beautiful Stump. The long journey in from the Lynn Knock will all of a sudden seem very worth while.

MOORINGS and FACILITIES on Spalding's river

In times past, Spalding, like Boston, was a prosperous local seaport situated where navigable water penetrated deep into a rich agricultural region. Now, only the ranks of elegant merchant houses and the remains of the occasional warehouse stand testimony to this former role. The river has long been locked on the outskirts of the town. Within the town it is a placid, overhung drain with shoal edges; outside the lock the river has silted to such an extent that a vessel drawing 5 feet (1·5m) would scarcely be able to reach it even on the biggest of tides. Even for shoal draught vessels there can be few attractions in penetrating as far as an industrial suburb of Spalding to find only shelving muddy banks to which to make fast. Spalding has turned its back on the sea to concentrate on its tulips and daffodils.

Fosdyke Bridge

Spalding water enthusiasts can maintain some kind of contact with life-giving tidewater, provided they have no mast to worry about, by basing their craft at Surfleet, some four or five miles lower down the Welland. Here, a major fen drain outfall has left a clough below the sluice some four hundred yards long, and it is sufficiently deep to allow a 5 feet draught boat floating time 1½ hours either side of high water. Local boatmen have constructed numerous substantial jetties on either side of the creek and the visitor can usually be assured of borrowing a mooring at one of these, or on the stone wall on the left hand side of the sluice, which contains a convenient ladder and has a reasonable bottom. The Ship Inn is at hand to provide refreshment for the weary Welland-worn mariner, and the more discerning drinker can find Bateman's Good Honest Ale one mile down the road at the site of the old railway station.

For masted vessels, Fosdyke bridge marks the limit of navigation on the Welland and it offers the same Honest brew at a pub of the same name – the Ship – as well as a good basic roadside store. The quayside of the old grain warehouse on the north bank has more than five feet of water at all states of the tide, though it is frequently occupied by a small coaster or barge, engaged in the fertilizer or grain trade.

Wainfleet Haven

On a stretch of coast where havens are worth their weight in gold, Wainfleet occupies a strategic location for the small boat skipper. The Wash ports of Lynn, Wisbech and Boston often surprise by their distance inland, and there must have been many occasions when a dying wind or inadequate tidal push have caught a Wash-bound skipper short on the tide. Since all the Wash ports are essentially tidal havens, then only Wainfleet offers

WAINFLEET HAVEN

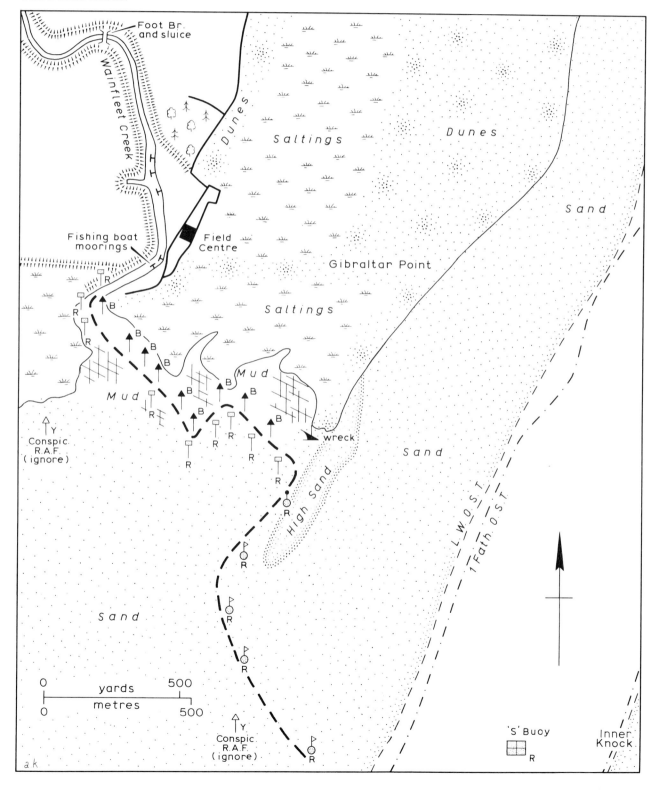

Foot Br. and sluice

Wainfleet Creek

Dunes

Saltings

Dunes

Sand

Fishing boat moorings

Field Centre

Gibraltar Point

Saltings

R

B

R

B

B

Mud

B

Mud

B

B

R

B

wreck

Sand

Y
Conspic.
R.A.F.
(ignore)

R

R

R

R

R

R

High sand

R

R

L.W.O.S.T.

1 Fath. O.S.T.

R

Sand

| 0 | yards | 500 |
| 0 | metres | 500 |

Y
Conspic.
R.A.F.
(ignore)

R

'S' Buoy

R

Inner Knock

a k

a safe and convenient alternative. Its situation, in the nook of Gibraltar Point, offers good shelter in the swatchway to make it a good low water anchorage; the actual entry to the haven, though tortuous, is well-marked, and protected even from easterly winds by the high drying beach of Gibraltar Point.

APPROACHES

The Boston Deeps, and its narrow north easterly extension, the Wainfleet Swatchway, provide good deep approaches and safe anchorage, provided reasonable vigilance is maintained. The route is buoyed by a green buoy to the south west (see chart no. 108) and by two red buoys through the Swatchway to the north east. In reasonable visibility, these buoys are visible one from the other, though unfortunately they are not lit, so it is a hazardous passage to undertake at night below half tide.

The Swatchway is flanked on its south eastern side by the Inner Knock, a hard sand which dries 7–8 feet (2·1–2·4m) at LWS. Several smaller sandbanks, among them the Outer Knock and Outer Dogs Head form a parallel series with swatchways between, but these may not be safely regarded as alternative approaches, for the least depths are not guaranteed to be over 2 feet (0·6m) and they are completely unmarked. The only safe approach from the east lies between the Inner Dogs Head and its larger south westerly extension, the Long Sand. Here is an important gat called the Parlour Channel which offers the vigilant mariner a useful alternative approach to Wainfleet. Two miles north of the South Well light buoy will be found the small and unlit buoys, one red (PA) and one green (PB), which mark the critical nesses at the eastern entrance to the Parlour Channel. In reasonable visibility, the much larger Parlour Fairway, PB(R) will be discerned 1½ miles to the west of these small buoys. Once this buoy is attained, anxieties can cease, for the Boston Deeps stretch safely to port and starboard. The Parlour Channel is an extremely strategic feature to any manoeuvre in this section of the Wash, for it has a least depth of 7 feet (2·1m) at LWS, but caution must be exercised owing to the narrowness of the channel, the steepness of the adjacent sands and the paucity of buoyage.

ENTRY

The entry channel to Wainfleet Haven is safe and well-marked but it is tortuous and subject to change in the lower section, so attention to pilotage instructions is essential. Entry can be effected with 5 feet (1·5m) of draught two hours either side of HWS and one hour either side of HWN, though strong southerly winds can prevent the neapest of tides from giving 5 feet (1·5m) in the creek even at HW.

The river mouth, as it is known, usually lies some 300 yards west or north west of the conspicuous 'S' buoy. The local yacht club attempts to keep a fairway buoy on station, but the bulk of the buoyage in the lower section is maintained by local fishermen for their own information. In general, it can be assumed that red buoys with topmarks are middle channel markers and that white buoys which seem to litter the surroundings are simply indicators of old buoy moorings which must be ignored.

The inner section of the haven is tortuous, but well marked by a series of port and starboard beacons, the former being surmounted by red cans, the latter by black triangular topmarks. It is essential to pass between the first port hand beacon and the turbulent end of the spit, despite the narrowness of the gap and the unpromising appearance of the water. Further into the creek, the channel becomes more obvious as the marsh is sufficiently high to be visible even at HWS.

MOORINGS

Moorings in Wainfleet Creek are all privately owned, but there are always some spare, and both the local fishermen and the yacht club members are very co-operative in helping the visitor find suitable moorings for a short stay. A phone call in advance to the local lifeboat coxwain, Paul Martin (☎ (0754) 3430) will greatly facilitate the mooring procedure. For the deep draughted boat, the fishing jetties are most suitable. These are the first moorings encountered on entry. Smaller boats are better advised to proceed further up the haven and tie up where there is jetty space. In general it may be assumed that where there is a jetty, then the bottom is of soft mud and of reasonable contour. There are no hazards.

FACILITIES

In the eighteenth century, Wainfleet is recorded as having a substantial coastal trade with Hull. Oats, sheepskins, horns, bones and sheep's foot oil were exported to the big city, while wine, tobacco, snuff, raisins, spices and exotic timber were imported. The visiting mariner can, therefore, be pardoned a gasp of astonishment as he surveys the marshland idyll of today. Wainfleet offers safety and a great deal of peace, but that is all. Gibraltar Point is a nature reserve, and the enthusiast can find all he wants in terms of marsh and dune vegetation, moth and bird life. The roisterer, however, will not find Wainfleet to his taste. Indeed, even the more conservative demands of the average cruising yachtsman cannot be easily met, though the Field Study Centre has water and toilets, and the local yacht club have installed a water standpipe on the bank and will make their clubhouse showers available on request.

More elaborate services are available in Skegness, (E.C. Thurs.), a surprisingly elegant and seasonally vibrant holiday resort some 3½ miles to the north along a good metalled road. In summer there is an infrequent but regular bus service between Skegness and Gibraltar Point. Alternatively, the ditch crawling mariner who is interested in maximum penetration to the historic heart of Wainfleet Haven can carry his dinghy around the sluice and row three or four miles to the old port and market town of Wainfleet which boasts the brewing of Bateman's Good Honest Ale and various other rural service activities.

Saltfleet

Men of the Lincolnshire marshlands have long been more concerned with keeping the sea from their reclaimed fields than with accommodating mariners and their vessels. The Lincolnshire coast, therefore, presents a fairly formidable face to seaward. Only in one place is there any chink in the armour of the steep dunes; that place is Saltfleet. There are eighteenth-century shipping records of *Godfrey's Cordial* and *Daffy's Elixir* (brands of opium water) being imported by the crateload at Saltfleet. In return, the presumably besotted farmers produced woad for the dyeworks of Hull and the West Riding.

Perhaps Saltfleet has deteriorated as a haven since the eighteenth century, or perhaps the requirements of mariners are rather more searching nowadays. Whatever the case, Saltfleet is no easy harbour of refuge and there are certain weather conditions which make it untenable. The author has entered Saltfleet under sail, in *Venture*, in an easterly Force 5. This must be about the limit of strength in which entry is advisable if there is any east in the wind at all. The coast is uncompromisingly straight and there is no shelter in the roadstead. The bar is high and dangerous, and the gap in it exceedingly narrow. But having said this, one must emphasise the other side of the coin; Saltfleet is an attractive haven and well worth a visit. Provided the entry is treated with the precision it deserves, and provided the weather conditions are good, it should present no problems to the cruising skipper.

APPROACHES (See Admiralty chart no. 107)

The Lincolnshire coast is rather featureless, and precise position is often difficult to determine. From Mablethorpe to Donna Nook, the crest of the dunes is dotted with the occasional clump of trees, the odd farmhouse and a few lookout towers. Saltfleet village can be discerned by its copse of trees, higher and thicker than any other copse on the coast. The haven lies about a quarter of a mile south of this clump of trees, but the mariner is advised to keep about three-quarters of a mile offshore when making this approach. The beach dries out this far from the coast, but it is a reasonably even slope and offers no traps provided vigilance with the soundings is kept. South of the harbour mouth, the sands reach out about a hundred yards further seaward than they do to the north. A danger zone buoy (Y, No.6) lies about a mile to the north east of the haven entrance, providing a nerve-wrackingly approximate confirmation of the other identifying features. Occasionally, the local boatmen place a fairway buoy directly off the entrance, but this feature cannot be relied on.

ENTRY

Lacking any natural protection, Saltfleet's entrance channel is vulnerable to changes which derive from the interplay of wind, sea state and fresh water. In general terms it can be stated that in winter, the channel tends to cut through the bar and disgorge the fresh water directly into the sea, whilst in summer the longshore drift tends to build the bar up and divert the channel to the south as indicated in the sketch map. It is advisable for visiting yachtsmen to make preliminary enquiry of the local boatman, Paul West (☎ 050 785 8178), who will give advice and pilotage services if required.

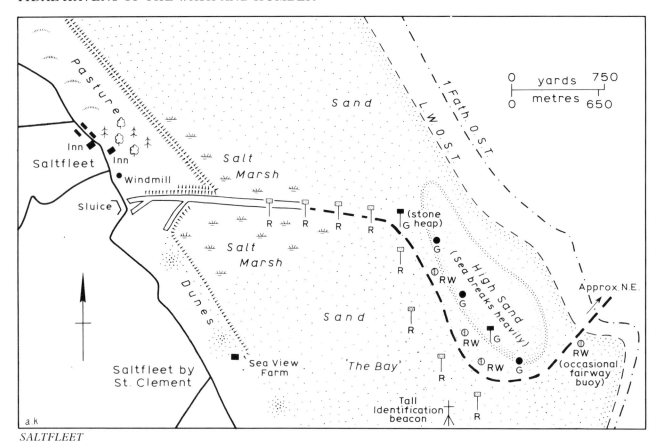

SALTFLEET

A vessel of 5 feet (1·5m) draught may enter Saltfleet on mean tides or above, although on mean tides a high water entry is recommended whilst one hour either side of springs is a sensible working margin. The best approach is from the north east, with the DZ buoy astern, and the harbour entrance can be approximately identified by the sighting of a large beacon with a cross topmark situated on the high sand inshore. On coming closer, the smaller buoys and beacons that mark the channel proper will be discerned and the vitally important requirement is to round the southernmost extremity of the bar before following the channel behind the bar in a northerly direction. The local fishermen and yachtsmen attempt, in the face of often violent sea conditions, to keep a system of buoyage in place, with port (R) and starboard (G) hand buoys and beacons on the channel edges and with mid-channel (RW) buoys to indicate the deepest parts of the creek. The port hand beacons mark the eastern edge of the high flat sand to landward which is a fairly stable feature. The problem with this section of the haven is that it runs extremely close behind the bar. There is no water on the bar at neap tides, but at springs, in an easterly, there is a turmoil of surf, even in the deep channel, which presents a fearsome prospect to the mariner unused to Saltfleet. In general, however, it can be said that provided the weather limits mentioned above are observed, then there is no danger of being rolled by the waves for the bar is sufficiently high to knock all the force out of the sea.

The sharp turn to port into the home straight of the haven marks the end of Saltfleet's problems. From here, the line of the channel goes straight in to the village, having been trained by brushwood banks in days of yore. High springs will cover the marshes on each hand, but there is sufficient evidence of where the banks lie to enable the mariner to sail without difficulty up the middle.

It is useful to note that the depth of water in the outer parts of the harbour is always greater than that in the creek. This means that, in quiet weather, the outer harbour behind the bar may be used as a temporary anchorage, either to await more water in the creek, or, if too late on the tide, to take the ground and wait through the low water period. Shoal draught vessels (i.e. those drawing less than 1m) can get into this 'bay', as it is locally, though not very convincingly, described, at half tide.

MOORINGS　　　　Most of the craft that are based at Saltfleet are shoal draughted, catamarans and bilge keels being the mode in sailing boats. They usually moor nose to the bank, stern to mooring buoys, on the southern bank of the haven, immediately below the fork. Visiting craft of this type will probably be able to pick up one of these moorings, temporarily vacated by its owner. Larger vessels, and those with more searching keels, are better advised to proceed directly up the main channel ignoring the two forks to the left, and to tie up along the south wall of the village sluice. The water authority does not like this, but it has never been known to turn anyone away provided they do not propose to leave the boat there for any length of time unattended. There is a slope of mud at the wall, and a mast rope is essential.

FACILITIES　　　　Saltfleet is a charming village and will delight the visiting yachtsman. The New Inn is a very old, and picturesque inn, which has recently been ruined by extensive renovation to cater for the caravan site which is discreetly hidden in the trees behind the pub. The beer is poor fare, but the New Inn's caravan enterprise has turned Saltfleet into a handy Calor gas refuelling station. The Crown, around the corner, offers poor beer and good cheer; even children are made heartily welcome. The post office, methodist church, small shops and filling station are clustered tightly around, making Saltfleet one of those rare places on the east coast where revictualling is not a major chore.

Tetney

In the late eighteenth century, market towns required access to navigable waters in order to remain prosperous. The export of agricultural and manufactured produce, and the import of coal to fuel the enterprises, were only feasible if navigable water could be utilised. In many respects, Louth was well-placed. Only ten flat miles from the sea, it did not require much investment in canal building; the river Lud provided a convenient route for canalisation, with a well-marked outfall at the mouth of the Humber opposite Spurn Head. Yet there were problems, and it was the persistence of these problems which finally spelled the decay and closure of the Louth Navigation, and the dismantling of the outfall lock at Tetney, so ingeniously constructed by the Hull engineer, Grundy. Today, the Louth Navigation is used as a land drain; the tidal limit has been moved a mile downstream, where a new drainage sluice has been constructed; all that remains of the Louth Navigation is Tetney Haven, a haven of very marginal utility to the cruising yachtsman.

There is a flourishing sailing club, the Humber Mouth Yacht Club (☎ Grimsby (0472) 812063) in Tetney Haven, and many distinguished yachtsmen have cut their teeth there. It is difficult, however, to imagine the circumstances under which a cruising yachtsman would ever want to visit the place. Bound down Humber, he would usually have no water in the haven by the time he arrived on the ebb tide; coming in from sea, the proximity of Grimsby, some six miles further upstream, would usually tempt him to a haven of more certainty, and with more facilities. It is possible, however, that a yacht is so late on the tide that Grimsby becomes unattainable. In this circumstance, Tetney is a viable alternative for those reluctant to attempt anchorage in the busy and fast-moving Humber. It is also possible that the skipper of a catamaran or a bilge-keeled boat, interested in collecting havens would actually set out to investigate Tetney for its own sake. For these people there are indeed safe moorings to be had, and there are no real difficulties to be encountered in attaining them.

APPROACHES
(See Admiralty chart no. 109, or ABP chart *Spurn Head to Barton Haven*)　　　　Haile Sand Fort, the southernmost of the first world war defence establishments for the Humber Mouth, is the obvious conspicuous landmark to make for. The fort just about dries out at LWS, but it is safe to sail quite close to it as there are no great irregularities in the shore line just at this point. The fairway buoy at the mouth of Tetney Haven is situated about half a mile upstream, in a north westerly direction, from the fort. Anchorage in the vicinity is not good, for the tide runs at three knots on springs, and the bottom is hard sand. The mariner is advised, therefore, to time his arrival at the beacon so as to ensure that there is plenty of water for entry, unless he has complete confidence in his ground tackle or unless he feels able to sail about and stem the tide as he waits.

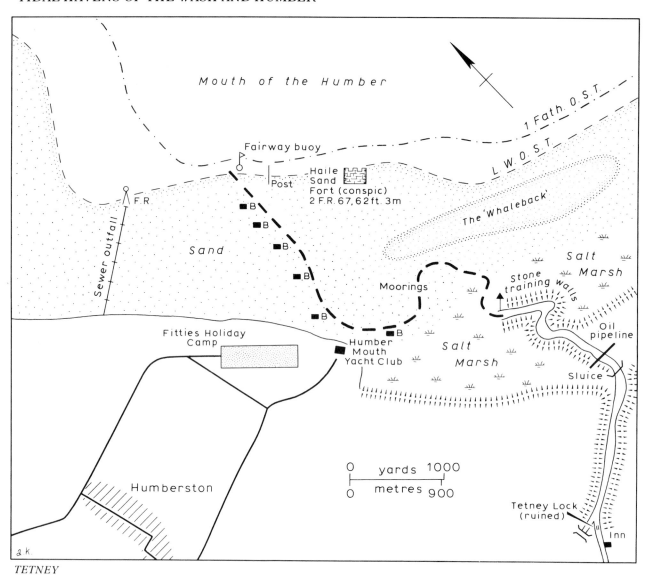

TETNEY

**ENTRY
and
MOORINGS**

A vessel drawing 5 feet (1·5m) may safely enter or leave Tetney Haven above half tide. The route followed by the deepest water is fairly straight and stable, and the yacht club members are diligent in adjusting the positions of the buoys to match any fluctuations. The fairway buoy, surmounted by a HMYC burgee, must first be identified, and the route up the haven from here is well marked by up to fifteen numbered black can buoys which must be left close to starboard coming in. These buoys are laid out in April and removed in October. From the last buoy, which is situated close to the yacht club, the deepest water can be picked out by the positions of the boat moorings. The visiting yachtsman is advised to either pick up a mooring, if one is spare, or to anchor in a position to clear other moored craft. Vessels take the sand at about half tide, but there is no risk of bumping, as by that time the haven is beautifully protected by the high drying sand to the north, known locally as the Whaleback.

The haven above this point, although important in the days of the Louth Navigation, is tortuous and dangerous. Stone-built training walls associated with recent land drainage schemes present a major hazard, not only by dint of channelling the flood tide into surges and eddies, but also because they cover well before HWS, presenting a nasty underwater obstacle to even the most vigilant of mariners. I have sailed Venture to the limit of navigation, which is a huge concrete oil pipe spanning the channel, but a series of near calamitous accidents with tidal surges persuaded me and my hard-pressed crew that the inclusion of pilotage details for this section of Tetney Haven would be a criminal invitation to disaster.

FACILITIES During the sailing season, from May until October, the steward and stewardess of the club live in their caravan on site, and will make any visitor extremely welcome, to the extent of opening up the club to provide showers, toilet and cooking facilities. During the same period of the year, the nearby Fitties holiday camp contains a shopping complex, with Calor gas, ironmonger, fish and chips and a seasonal tavern. The club itself, however, provides convivial bar facilities on Wednesday evenings and at weekends, and the warmth of the welcome here can go a long way to countermand the chilling effect of what is a rather bleak stretch of coast on a grey evening.

Perhaps the essence of Tetney Haven is the cockles and samphire. Nowhere to my knowledge do the cockles grow so big and in such profusion. Fifteen minutes on the Tetney marsh with a rake and net will yield cockles in almost commercial proportions. A boiling of cockles, lightly vinegared, a bunch of fresh samphire, and a summer sunset, can make Tetney a rewarding place.

Grimsby

The Italianate Victorian masterpiece of Grimsby hydraulic lock tower has long been the symbol of homecoming for trawlermen. Ever since the coming of the railway and the construction of Grimsby docks enabled the English fishing industry to increase its scale and exploit the rich harvests of the Silver Pits and Dogger Bank, Grimsby has been one of the two principle deep sea trawling ports of Britain. Yet the town has never turned its back on small boats. Variety is the keynote of Grimsby's fishing industry, and to this day the fish docks house smacks and seine netters as well as middle and deep sea trawlers. This penchant for variety seems also to have seeped through into the commercial docks, where the ABP are unusually solicitous towards the small boat skipper. This is fortunate, for Grimsby, by location and by facilities, occupies a central and strategic position in the cruising ground covered by this pilot.

APPROACHES
(See Admiralty chart no. 1188 or ABP chart *Spurn Head to Barton Haven*)

From the sea, the approach to Grimsby is straightforward. The deep water channel is well buoyed and lit, and small boat skippers can use far more of the lower Humber than is offered by the channel, even at low water. Indeed, there are no mid-channel obstacles below Grimsby, and the only underwater hazards occur near either shore, where the beaches have some nasty protuberances which are nevertheless very evident on the charts.

Approaching from up-Humber is slightly more problematical. Up to two hours each side of LWS, craft drawing up to 5 feet (1·5m) may use the Burcom Flats, a shallow depression between the Burcom Sand and the shore. Care must be taken, especially on the ebb, not to ground on the Burcom, and a good guide can be had, by both day and night, from the beacon on the end of the Pyewipe outfall, a mile and a half to westward of the west pier. From a point 200 yards to seaward of the beacon, a course straight to the pier is one which will give the deepest water across the Burcom Flats.

A craft coming down Humber too late on the tide to risk the Burcom Flats will be forced to round the Burcom Sand. This involves going down the main channel almost as far as the lower Burcom Float (precisely how far must be determined by the individual and his chart), and this necessitates punching the last of the ebb into the Royal Dock Basin. Although the tide at Grimsby is not nearly so strong as in the upper reaches, the mariner must expect three knots on springs, so he would be wise to have a good engine or a stiff fair breeze to assist him.

ENTRY
and
MOORINGS

There are two mooring possibilities in Grimsby, in the Fish Dock or in the commercial docks. Yachts unable or unwilling to lower masts must opt for the fish Dock, where the Grimsby Cruiser Association provides pontoon facilities immediately to starboard upon entering the dock, (call Ch 9 or 18). There is here a small marina with toilets and showers available. The Fish Dock is open on a free flow arrangement for two hours either side of HW, so this is clearly the most convenient mooring in Grimsby, albeit at considerable remove from any facilities.

Visitors without masts, or with lowering ones, have another option at Grimsby Marina in the commercial docks. Entry to the tidal outer basin of the Royal Docks, (VHF Ch 9 or 18) presents no problems, for the entrance is clearly marked by day and night, the tide is slack in the lee of the piers and there is sufficient water even at LWS to get alongside a wall. A sojourn in the basin can be a hazardous experience in bad weather, for waves and wash from pilot boats can cause abrasion. The outer (western) pier and the old disused (eastern) lock pit provide alternative temporary moorings in northerly and southerly winds respectively, but in a north easterly there is little respite. It is undoubtedly advisable to proceed through the locks into the docks as quickly as possible.

A 'pen', as the locking procedure is locally called, is available 3½ hours before high water. The dock gates are next opened when a level is made, from two hours to one hour before high water, depending on the size of the tide and amount of running off that has been undertaken over the low water period. The gates remain open for unimpeded ingress and egress until high water, when they are closed. One more pen is available, either in or out, at 2½ hours after high water, after which no access is possible across the low water period.

Grimsby

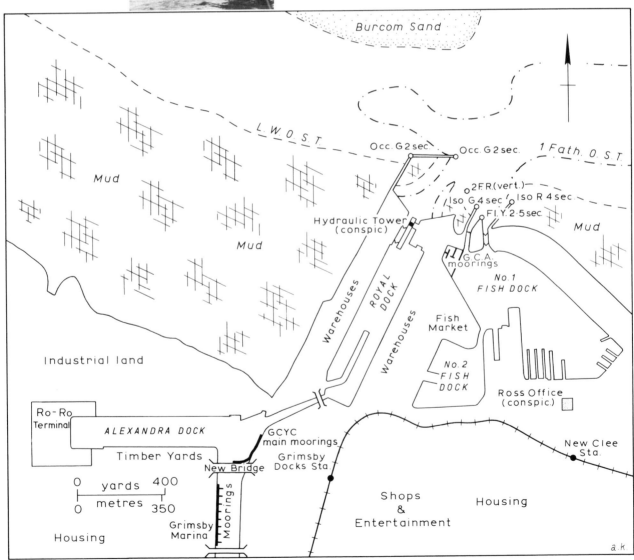

GRIMSBY

The Grimsby and Cleethorpes Yacht club have their moorings at the east end of Alexandra Dock, but there are no visitors' berths. Visitors must proceed under the new road bridge (headroom 10ft. to 20ft.) to Grimsby Marina (☎ 0472 360404) where are situated by far the best appointed and best located mooring facilities in the port.

FACILITIES

Grimsby is not a town of any great interest, nor are its buildings of any architectural merit. It does, however, offer the cruising yachtsman a complete range of facilities. He can eat, drink, watch cinema, get fuel, buy gas, restock with charts and chandlery. He could probably arrange to have his boat rebuilt if necessary, for there are engineers, ship-wrights and sailmakers in abundance on the Fish Docks. And in its own bleak way, Grimsby has charm and interest. The cries of the fish merchant, the clatter of wooden clogs, the sounds of Danish spoken freely in the shops and taverns – all these make Grimsby gloriously polyglot; it is to be hoped that the decline in the fishing industry does not rob it of its charm.

North Killingholme

The Lincolnshire bank of the Humber, downstream of Barton, has never offered the truly rural aspect presented by the farmlands of Holderness on the Yorkshire side. The local clays have long been intensively utilised for building materials, and the Humber shore is studded with the chimneys of tileries and brickworks. The development of Grimsby haven by the Manchester, Sheffield and Lincolnshire railway in the mid 19th century

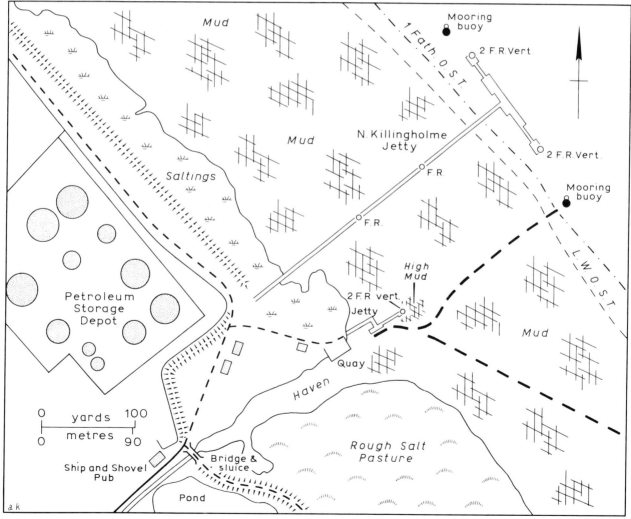

NORTH KILLINGHOLME

gave rise to the commercial dock system as we know it today, and when to this was added the installations and industries associated with deep sea fishing, a solid urban ingredient had indeed been dropped into the preindustrial scene. Yet there was something manageable and acceptable about the scale of industrial and urban development. Even the construction of Immingham Docks in the early 20th century by the Great Central Railway Company did not altogether destroy the essentially human scale of industrial and commercial activity. This part of Lincolnshire, in the 1920s, must still have offered a low and local profile, with small muddy havens serving the commercial needs of the villages situated some way inland away from the marshy foreshore – the Killingholmes, East Halton and Stallingborough. In the background, the rising ground of the Lincolnshire Wolds provided a prominent backdrop to an essentially local and isolated slice of early 20th century England.

The development of Immingham Dock, however, was a harbinger of drastic change. The deep water advantages of this bight in the lower Humber were recognised by the railway company in their search for a good spot from which to export Yorkshire and Nottinghamshire coal. It was only the decline in the coal exports which caused stagnation in the twenty years or so after the construction of the dock. The fundamental advantages of flat, open land next to deep tidewater could only lie dormant for a short time. By the 1930s, jetties were being built near South and North Killingholme havens to supplement the facilities of Immingham for the import and storage of petroleum and fuel oil, for both inland distribution and ship bunkering. Between Grimsby and Immingham chemical factories sprang up, belching their noxious fumes into the once pure sea air of the Humber estuary. During the 1950s and 1960s these developments burgeoned. To the south of Immingham Docks a huge oil jetty was built, capable of receiving tankers drawing up to 60 feet (18 metres). Crude oil landed here is refined at the two oil refineries built during the 1960s on the open land between Immingham and Killingholme. In the early 1970s, to the north of Immingham Docks and completely obliterating South Killingholme Haven, there was constructed a bulk cargo terminal, equipped to export coal and to import iron ore for the furnaces of Scunthorpe. The whole area was transformed into a smoking, smelly chemical complex – industry at a scale which reduces man to mouse. In the middle of all this there is but one place for small boats – North Killingholme Haven.

APPROACHES,
ENTRY
and
MOORING

The haven lies hard on the downstream side of the northernmost of the several ship jetties which project into the Humber upstream of Grimsby. It is therefore conspicuous by day and night. But whilst the big jetty may facilitate identification, it does to some extent impede approaches, especially on the full ebb, for a vessel is liable to be swept well past the haven entrance through having to give the jetty sufficient clearance.

The haven can be safely approached at a variety of angles, as indicated in the sketch chart. Coming downstream, it is necessary to round the tanker mooring buoy before laying a course for the haven entrance. Approaching from downstream, a finer angled approach can be made to suit wind and tide conditions and to ensure that slacker water is gained before the flood tide threatens to set the vessel on to the ship jetty. The shore mud slopes evenly so there are no navigational hazards.

The haven itself is a poor affair and only suitable for shoal draught vessels. The stream from the sluice has cut a tortuous channel through the mud and even if it were possible to describe the sinuosities it would be of little value to the non-local boatman. Fortunately for the utility of the haven a barge jetty has been constructed out from the upstream side of the entrance. Barges and other working river craft are usually tied up to this jetty, but the mud bottom at this point is soft and flat and it is nearly always possible to lie outside them. The outer end of the jetty has a skirt of high mud around it, as indicated on the sketch chart. It is advisable, therefore, to give the first 20 feet (6m) or so a wide berth before coming alongside. A mooring against the rest of the jetty or outside a barge can be reached with a vessel drawing 5 feet (1·5m) 2½ hours either side of spring highs and 2 hours either side of neaps.

FACILITIES

There is little to attract the visitor to Killingholme Haven. The presence of a havenside pub, the Ship and Shovel, is a feature rare enough in this cruising ground to merit attention, and it is a facility well utilised by local inshore fishermen taking a rest between tides. But it is a plastic pub, purveying top pressure beer to a captive market of oil industry workers, and it really does very little to alleviate the desolate and malodorous scene. The village is three or four miles inland and the walk is not pleasant. There are no shops nearby. Killingholme Haven simply hangs on, a beaten-up remnant of the world we have lost.

East Halton (Skitter Haven)

Any regular Humber mariner, homeward bound for Hull on a flood tide, will know the frustration of falling short. The distance from Spurn or Donna Nook is so great that a fickle wind can easily prove inadequate for the task, despite the fiercely reliable tide. For a craft without an engine, or with an engine unequal to the task of pushing over the ebb, such an event can be sorely trying. An anchorage in the Humber is at best uncomfortable and nerve wracking, at the worst, dangerous. A return to Grimsby can be long and tedious, and there may be no chance of entering the docks by the time the basin is reached. In such circumstances, the Skitter Haven is a godsend. It is safe and it is close enough to Hull to make the task on the next tide a swift and certain one. Even for the Brough bound skipper, Skitter can be of use, for he can usually be assured of more than two hours of flood after lifting off on the next tide.

APPROACHES,
ENTRY
and
MOORINGS

Skitter Haven is situated at the point where the concrete sea wall, stretching NW from N Killingholme jetty, gives way to a more gentle grass-covered one. The 'nesses' on either side have their quota of stones and mud falling sharply away, but they offer no real hazard. From 2½ hours before HW entry can be made. It is best to approach the haven from south of centre, to enter more or less mid way between the two nesses, and then to steer for the northern side, where the deep water curves round the bank to the sluice gates at the innermost end. Local boatmen attempt to maintain a beacon on the high ness of mud on the southern side of the entrance. There are half a dozen small jetties in the

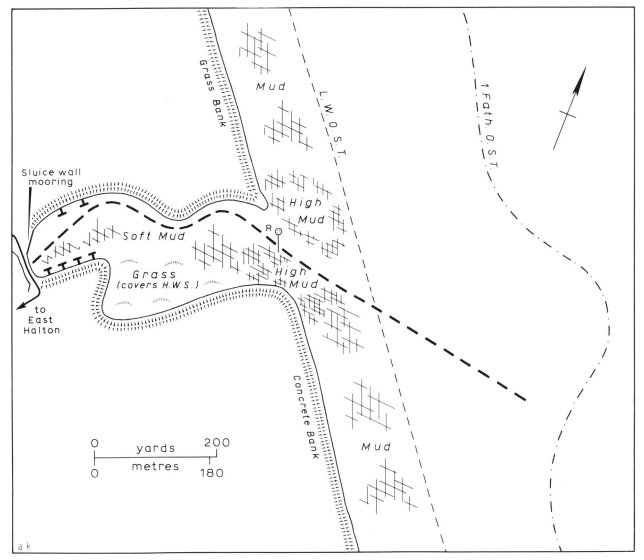

EAST HALTON

haven, all owned by local people for private use, but if one is temporarily vacated, the visitor is welcome to use it and the mud is everywhere soft. Failing this, another mooring is afforded by the northern wall of the sluice, though care must be taken to keep as close to the sluice gate as possible, to avoid a steep mound of mud at the northern end. Here the bottom is harder so a mast rope is advisable.

FACILITIES   East Halton is slightly over two miles from the haven, but the fact that good, metalled roads lead right down to the sluice makes these two miles much less daunting than is often the case at more wild and marshy havens. A walk through the mellow rural countryside of North Lincolnshire can be a delight in good weather, and the village of East Halton offers a good selection of village facilities – grocer, post office, public house and chip shop.

New Holland

New Holland, as anyone who has ever been there will immediately realise, was not established as a colony by Dutchmen fleeing religious persecution or seeking freedom to develop their weaving skills. It was, in the early 19th century no more than a sluice outlet in a dark and remote corner of Barrow parish which offered 'advantages for the debarkation of smuggled goods, more especially for Holland's gin, and it was notoriously used as such.' The settlement that the visitor sees today was developed by the Manchester, Sheffield and Lincolnshire Railway in anticipation of a commercial boom that never materialised. The promise of passenger traffic across the Humber to Hull encouraged them to terminate their railway line on a pier of magnificent proportions which stretched out across the low tide mudflats to a floating pontoon to and from which the ferries plied, albeit with occasional difficulty, at all stages of the tide. The promise of commercial traffic encouraged them to excavate a dock with wharfage for a dozen or more vessels. The anticipated labour demands of both these enterprises encouraged them to build a small company town with a hotel, the Yarborough, of grandiose proportions. All these features still stand to this day, yet New Holland has the atmosphere and accoutrements of an industrial archaeology museum rather than a place with any commercial or residential viability for the fourth quarter of the twentieth century. Only a few years ago it was full of fascination for the visiting yachtsman: the coal fired paddle steamer being fuelled by trolleys from the coal trucks at the pier end; the trains creeping along the pier between New Holland town and New Holland Pier stations; the cars, alien intrusions on to a pure 19th century scene, wobbling precariously along the unguarded platform to the waiting ferry. All these are now gone. Timber and coal ships still use the dock, and the pier has been converted into a bulk cargo wharf, but New Holland basically just lies there rotting, the hulks of ancient sailing ships and the neglected square of company houses serving as a poignant reminder of an optimistic and dignified era that has gone for ever.

APPROACHES,   New Holland dock, situated fifty yards downstream of the base of the conspicuous ferry
ENTRY   pier, may be entered with 5 feet (1·5m) of draught upward of half tide. In any case, if
and   there is sufficient water to permit entry, then the approaches present no problems, for
MOORINGS   sands in the middle and near the banks are sufficiently covered to pass over easily. Care must be taken, if approaching from downstream on the flood, to avoid overshooting and being carried under the pier by the tide. As with most piers and jetties on the Humber, however, the force of the tide slackens considerably as the banks are approached, so no real difficulty should be encountered provided the danger is realised.

The mud is everywhere soft, so that moorings are problem free and no mast ropes are required. Cargo vessels often unload along the eastern quay, so care must be taken to avoid interference with this work. The dock is private and mooring is by courtesy of the timber firm who lease it, so the visitor must conform to mooring instructions given by the employees of the firm.

FACILITIES   Despite its unprepossessing ambience in the middle of a timber dock, a mooring at New Holland offers certain advantages over some of the more picturesque, but more remote Humber havens. The town, or village as it more really is, is close to hand and boasts two pubs, a railway station, shops, garage, post office and fish and chips. In the days when it was a railhead and ferry terminal the place had a gaunt significance in Hum-

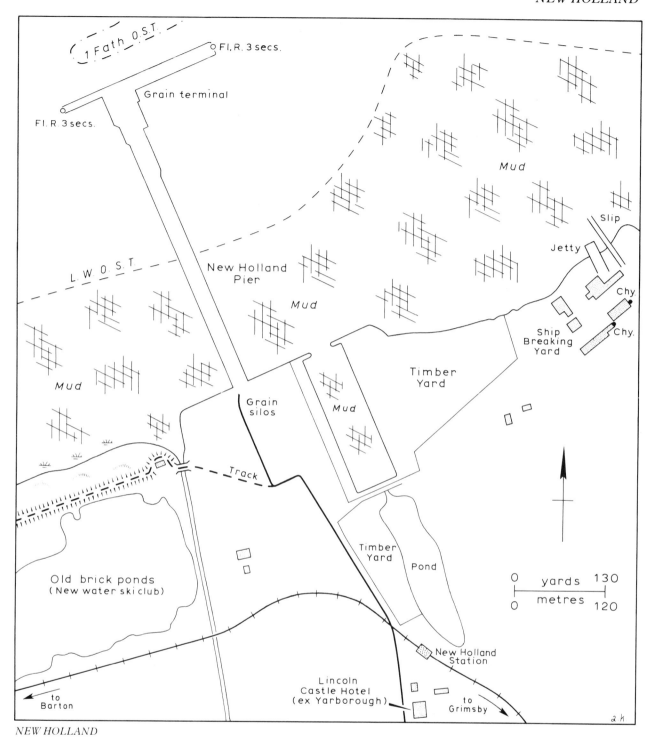

NEW HOLLAND

ber cruise planning. To ignore it could involve vast amounts of time and money travelling round by Scunthorpe and Goole. Now the Humber bridge stands proudly a few miles upstream. New Holland can be conveniently ignored and it usually is. It used to be a fascinating living museum of bygone systems. Now it is a dead one, and full of sadness.

Barrow upon Humber

There is something rather nice about Barrow Haven. On the face of it, there is not a great deal to recommend it: the village, though picturesque, is two miles away; it has no strategic utility which could set it off from other havens near at hand on both banks of the river. Yet it remains a firm favourite. It has a very definite aura of the past, nestling among the long, low pantiled roofs of its brickworks and tileries. It exudes a peace which makes it an ideal spot to head for on a long summer's evening.

APPROACHES, ENTRY and MOORINGS

The low bank of the Humber between New Holland Pier and Barton chemical works seems from a distance to be unbroken. Just over a mile to the west of the pier, however, are the two brick chimneys of Barrow tilery, and the haven is situated some two hundred yards upstream of these chimneys. There are no problems with approaches; if there is enough water to contemplate the haven there are no dangers in the offing. A vessel drawing 5 feet (1·5m) can enter 2½ hours either side of spring tides and 1½ hours either side of neaps.

An approach slightly east of centre of the haven entrance and aimed at the down-haven end of the new concrete quay will lead between the two steep offshore mudbanks. Leading marks, with red circular topmarks, and situated just down-haven of the new commercial quay, are used to indicate to timber ships the deepest approaches, and up-haven of the quay the deepest water is found in the centre of the haven all the way to the bridge and beyond.

The new quay is commercial, so care must be taken not to obstruct any activity that is taking place, or is about to take place. On the numerous occasions when the quay is empty, however, the visiting yachtsman will find it a very good mooring. The bottom is of flat, soft mud so that no mast ropes are required, and there are two extremely sound ladders built into the quay. Farther up the haven there are several mooring jetties, all privately owned, but temporary accommodation can usually be secured. If the place looks crowded, (though crowding is a relative term and Barrow is always a picture of solitude), the big jetties immediately below and above the slipway are the best bet. Larger vessels usually berth here, and the configuration of the bottom is such that a craft will remain upright however far out into the haven stream she has to lie. There is no danger of a boat sliding or leaning awkwardly against its neighbour at this spot. A small mooring fee is usually levied by the landowner.

Barrow Haven excluding peace

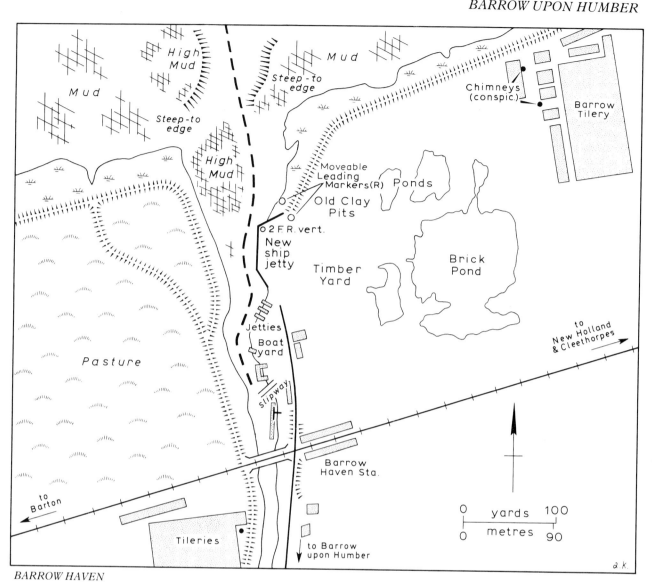

BARROW HAVEN

FACILITIES   Water is laid on to the top on the big jetty – a facility for filling up which is quite rare in this rather primitive cruising ground. Beer and other refreshments are available at the Haven Inn, a half a mile up the road beyond the railway station, but it is an inn which has developed a reputation as a night spot, with the concomitant battery of top pressure beers, basket meals and cacophonous rock groups which harmonise rather poorly with the Victorian scene outside. A walk to the village is well worth while. Here there are general stores, a post office and two or three less strident taverns which afford more traditional hospitality to the visiting yachtsman.

One curious feature of Barrow Haven is its railway station. Stretching away towards Barton in the west and New Holland in the east is a switchback single track railway which looks incapable of supporting any rolling stock. Along the line, however, there jolts an hourly train which can serve the very useful purpose of trundling crew members away to shop in Barton.

Barton upon Humber

Upstream from the industrial sprawl of Grimsby and Immingham, the south bank of the Humber is almost devoid of settlements and service centres of a substantial size. The one exception is Barton, formerly a market town of some importance, but now without market and delightfully decayed – a fascinating mixture of substantial town houses, cottages and shops. The small chemical works on the Humber bank renders the maritime prospect of Barton something short of idyllic, but it continues to be a place of much charm. The completion of the Humber bridge in 1981 was seen by some as a blow to Barton's character and independence. As yet, however, there is no evidence that it is turning into a suburb of Hull. The folks of Barton use the bridge and the city to their advantage but continue to turn their backs on it all when it suits their mood.

APPROACHES, ENTRY and MOORINGS

Barton Haven is made conspicuous by the tall concrete tower of the chemical works a hundred yards to the east of the entrance. The works has a large private jetty which is usually vacant, but it is not a very placid mooring, and the haven is preferable. There are no difficulties in the approaches or entry, for the Humber mud slopes evenly away from the shore and the channel is dead straight, as indicated in the sketch. The problem lies in the depth of water and in the restricted mooring space. The deepest water lies along the eastern quay, and a vessel drawing 5 feet (1·5m) can reach this quay 2 hours either side of springs and one hour either side of neaps.

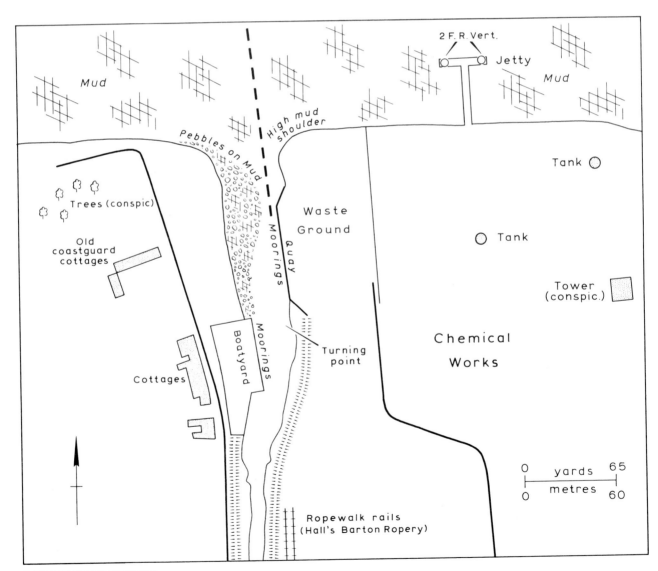

BARTON UPON HUMBER

Barton Waterside

A mooring on the east quay, though at advantage in terms of depth, is disadvantaged in two ways. In the first place, the stream bottom is relatively hard, so mast rope procedures are advisable for boats with keels. Second, the walk to facilities is quite long, and fraught with some difficulty in circumventing a factory fence. When more water is available, it is infinitely preferable to proceed up haven a short distance to Hammond's boatyard on the west quay. The advantages of good wall ladders, soft mud, less tidal range and direct road access to facilities are well worth the small mooring fee levied.

FACILITIES

Barton (E.C. Thurs) is an ideal service centre for a cruising yachtsman. Its facilities are obviously far more limited than those of Hull or Grimsby, but they are clustered and convenient in a way often lacking in the larger towns. The railway station, with a train service to Grimsby and bus services to Hull and Scunthorpe, is half a mile up the haven. The town itself is centred just a short distance inland from the station. Here a full range of shops, cafes, pubs and banks is available. Barton has a lengthy maritime tradition, it being the original ferry terminal for the Hull ferries. The brick and tile ropewalk of the old ropery provides a charming front to the eastern side of the haven. But, sadly, Barton has turned its back on the Waterside and looks inland or towards the bridge. It is left to the visiting yachtsman, cruising alone or with one other boat, to invoke the bygone atmosphere of Barton Waterside.

Ferriby Sluice

Ferriby Sluice is, without doubt, the most useful and strategic of all the Humber havens. The river Ancholme, draining the twenty-five mile long vale between the Lincoln Edge and the Lincolnshire Wolds, has a much more substantial catchment area than any of the other streams and drains which sluice out into the Humber. As a consequence, there is a much greater volume of water discharged, and this is reflected in the wide and deep channel scoured through the mud between the sluice and the Humber stream. When to this unusual utility of the haven is added the quality of the freshwater moorings of the Ancholme, and the attractive, if limited, inland cruising ground which the river provides, then the popularity of Ferriby Sluice with the boat owners of North Lincolnshire becomes very understandable.

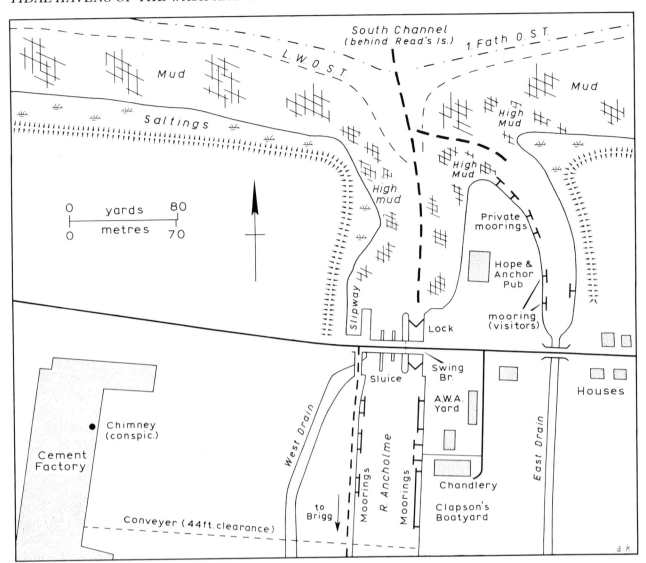

FERRIBY SLUICE

APPROACHES
and
ENTRY

The south channel of the Humber, passing to the south of Read's Island, always has deep water. Sometimes the Humber sands shift so as to provide a more direct channel for shipping in the wider section to the north of the island, and at such times the buoyed channel may be moved to the north, but the situation of the south channel, on the outside of a big bight, ensures constant deep water which gives guaranteed access to the haven at Ferriby Sluice. The position of the haven is easily identifiable by day and night, owing to the conspicuous, if rather obnoxious, existence of a large cement works immediately to the west of it.

Vessels drawing 5 feet (1·5m) may enter the haven and gain access to the lock pit 4 hours either side of high water, and at neap tides it frequently occurs that access can be had right across the low water period. The contours of the haven are such, however, that care must be taken to avoid the high shoulders of mud at all states of the tide. Entry is simple and straight, as indicated in the sketch chart, though note must be made of the speed of the flood tide off the haven mouth. At springs, this can attain a speed of 8 knots, and irregularities of the bed force fast-moving water into whirlpool-like convolutions which can be rather vexing for the incoming skipper attempting to negotiate precisely the projecting mud shoulders. I have on one occasion deposited *Venture* on the shoulder and on another occasion been swept past completely in a fickle breeze totally unequal to the task. In the first circumstance, the incoming tide eventually lifted her off, permitting a safe if sheepish approach to the lock; the other mishap necessitated a hasty revision of cruising plan and Winteringham was unanimously voted a superior spot to spend the night. The ebb tide offers no such alternatives, but it is less fierce and gives a more convenient angle of approach to the haven.

Ferriby Sluice and Read's Island

MOORINGS

It is not advisable to moor outside the locks at Ferriby Sluice. The walls of the sluice itself are free of projections, but the hazards of the sluicing process, the hardness of the sills below and the unscalable heights of the walls at low water make them an unpleasant and hazardous proposition. There is a subsidiary creek to the east where boat owners have erected a number of substantial jetties, but they are usually occupied by local craft, and double mooring on the steep mud slopes is unwise. Two of them, as indicated on the sketch chart, belong to the publican, and visitors are welcome if the berths are free.

The lock keepers are on duty from 7.30am to 4.00pm seven days a week, and they are available by arrangement at all other times, so it is a penny pinching skipper indeed who would set his face against the excellent mooring facilities that lie within, just to save the very reasonable locking and mooring fees. In the lock entrance is hung, during the summer months, a wire to which boats can be made fast whilst waiting for the lock keeper to open the gates and the bridge. Once inside, the visitor will be informed by the lock keeper as to where to moor in what is an understandably popular and normally crowded mooring. Moorings are available on both the east and west banks and belong either to Clapson's Boatyard (☎ Barton (0652) 635620) or the National Rivers Authority (☎ Barton (0652) 635219). A pipeline from a quarry to the cement factory crosses the Ancholme about three hundred yards from the sluice, giving a clearance of 44 feet (13m). Further up river, warning notices indicate that electric wires give only 30 feet (9m) clearance.

FACILITIES

Ferriby Sluice is an unprepossessing place when one's focus of interest moves away from the water, the moorings and boatyard. The cement factory presides greyly over a linear straggle of houses, and the only facilities are a garage and a telephone. Even the village of South Ferriby, a mile away to the east on the scarp slope of the Wolds, offers only a small general store. The saving grace of the place as far as apres-sail activities are concerned, is the Hope and Anchor, a basic and spacious public house with good beer, a friendly clientele and a landlord with a keen interest in boats.

Winteringham Haven

By far the most picturesque of the Humber havens, Winteringham has long been a firm favourite for a top of the tide crossing from Brough or for an upstream weekend from Hull or Grimsby. Recognising its potential, the Humber Yawl club several years ago purchased some land along the haven side with a view to providing, for their south bank members, similar facilities to those which have long been available at Brough. The project lay dormant for years, and up to 1976 the visitor to this charming haven could be assured of as much peace and solitude as he could wish. At the limited moorings of the old jetty, two boats constituted a crowd, so few people were prepared to take the risk. Since then, the Humber Yawl Club has developed its investment. No doubt such a move is in the in-

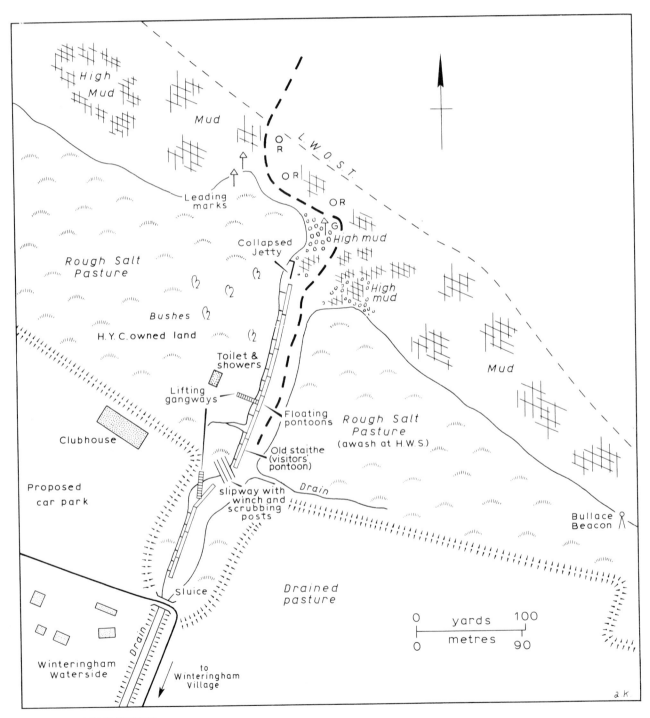

WINTERINGHAM HAVEN

terests of boating and is consequently to be welcomed. I cannot help feeling, however, a twinge of wistfulness for those lovely frosty winter weekends when *Venture* lay in deep solitude on the moonscape mud against a rickety staithe, at one with the past.

APPROACHES,
ENTRY
and
MOORINGS

Entry may be made with 5 feet (1·5m) of draught 2 hours either side of HWS and 1 hour either side of HWN. The Humber Yawl Club maintains a system of leading marks and buoyage to mark the entrance. The leading marks indicate the best initial approach and the series of red buoys and perches mark the port hand limits of the channel. The steep high spit which necessitates a sharp turn to port (see sketch map) is marked by a beacon with a green starboard topmark.

The club have laid down extensive floating pontoons on the western side of the haven, accessible by gangplanks. Visitors are requested to moor to the pontoon section immediately in front of the old market staithe, though the club mate, Mr. Dave Brammel (☎ 0724 734521) may offer alternative suggestions depending on which of the home-based boats are in residence. At all places in the haven, boats will sink almost to their marks in soft, comfortable mud.

FACILITIES

The Humber Yawl Club has constructed a slipway which features both winch and leaning posts which are available to visitors in emergency. The clubhouse is comfortable, though non-licensed, and has toilets and showers which are freely available to visitors. The village of Winteringham, lazily sprawling on the rising land half a mile or so inland of the haven, has rather more to offer and is one of the features which make a visit to this haven so worth while. Its houses have an old world charm, its stores and post office are convenient and its public house, the Ferry Boat, is hospitable. The throngs of aluminium masts in the haven may only be a tenuous link with the days when keels plied to and from the market jetty, but Winteringham still evokes in a tantalizing, intangible way some unspecific earlier decade.

Behind the Humber

The source of the Humber could be the cruising yachtsman's Holy Grail. On arriving at Trent Falls, he could legitimately claim to have found it, for here the Trent and the Ouse converge to spawn a river far grander than their combined efforts would seem to merit. Yet it is very unlikely that a visitor, having taken the trouble to navigate the length of the Humber, would content himself with making Winteringham or Broomfleet his ultimate cruising objective, fascinating as these charming villages may be. The Humber watershed stretches from Donna Nook to Spurn in a wide arc through Louth, Leicester, Birmingham, Stoke on Trent, Todmorden, Hawes, Richmond and Driffield. Indeed, it comes close to taking Scarborough from the rear. It contains three National Parks, an abundance of mellow agricultural countryside, some of the greatest of our English cities, and a myriad small industrial towns, each with its own unique flavour. When this is added to the bonus that, of all the English watersheds, this is the one most comprehensively threaded by navigable water, then its lure becomes obvious. Only Neptune himself could turn round at Trent Falls and go back to the sea.

A description of these waters is, however, clearly outside the scope of this pilot. Techniques are different, problems of mooring and locking are different, and the whole flavour of the cruising ground is different. Moreover, other publications exist which cover the water, albeit in a piecemeal form. The tidal waters of the Ouse and Trent, together with the industrial canalways towards Leeds, Wakefield and Sheffield, are dealt with by Derek Bowskill in his *Northeast Waterways* (Imray).

A necessary adjunct is the series of sketch charts produced by the Trent Boating Association and available from T. Pattison, 16 Baker Avenue, Arnold, Notts. These provide, for the tidal sections of the Ouse and Trent, information for the cruising skipper concerning tide times, tidal bores, mooring possibilities and shoal ground on these two mighty rivers. Other Humber linkages – the Ancholme, the Hull valley to Driffield, the Derwent – are most comprehensively dealt with by the publications of the amateur restoration groups who continue to energetically improve their local navigational heritage. Suffice it to say that, notwithstanding the vigour of the natural elements, the area immediately behind the Humber is a thrilling and enjoyable cruising ground.

51

Broomfleet

Broomfleet is strictly for the yachtsman who is enthusiastic about visiting quaint, interesting and pleasant places; it has no strategic utility as do some of the Humber havens. Indeed, it is not really a haven at all, for it is simply the point where the Market Weighton canal makes its outfall through the Humber sea wall. For some 200 years the canal remained open. At first, it was constructed to give water access to Market Weighton, but it never quite reached Market Weighton, so was of minimal importance in its upper reaches. The commercial importance of the canal rested largely with the brickworks built on the canal side at Newport and Broomfleet. Keels and sloops served these enterprises until the 1950s. After that, although it did not lose navigational rights until 1971, the canal served as a major field drain for this eastern part of the Vale of York. Proposals to remove the sluice and lock in favour of more modern sluice equipment, however, led to vigorous protests from the industrial archaeologists, for it is a unique example of an eighteenth century two-way self-acting sluice. A preservation order was placed on it which served to protect it during the lean years until 1980, when the Yorkshire Water Authority, new custodians of the canal, restored the lock and sluices to an efficient working condition whilst at the same time retaining their historical external appearance. The navigation is once more open, though the bridge at the lock prevents it being of any use to masted boats, and even for motor cruisers the hinterland is too linear and limited for it to be a popular waterway.

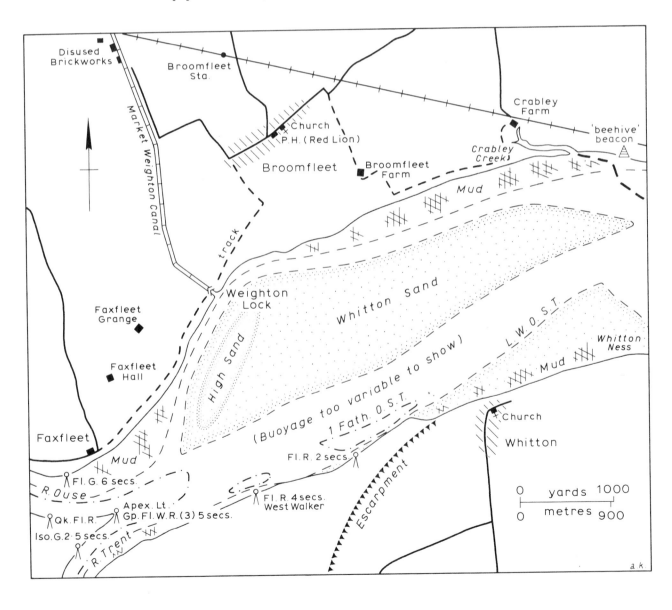

APPROACHES,
ENTRY
and
MOORINGS

Between the Whitton Sand to the south, and the Yorkshire bank to the north, a curving channel of relatively deep water is kept scoured by the tide. This channel may be entered from east or west by a vessel drawing 5 feet (1·5m) on all but the lowest of spring tides. The eastern end of the Whitton Sand tends to migrate, so close attention to the latest edition of the ABP chart is essential, but no difficulties should be encountered with the manoeuvre.

Some 300 yards upstream of the conspicuous red and white 'beehive' beacon is the entrance to Crabley Creek, a beautiful but little used haven which gives access to Broomfleet and Ellerker villages. Vessels drawing 5 feet can use the creek happily on mean tides or higher, but it is unused and unmarked, so pilotage instructions are impossible. The visitor is advised to inspect the ground prior to arrival or to edge in early between the surrounding mudbanks before they cover and create confusion. Inside the creek, which is navigable for about 400–500 yards, there is a variety of soft mud mooring places with grassy banks, reeds, wild life and numerous sheep.

On smaller tides, or without the leisure to make preliminary reconnaissance, the yachtsman is better advised to proceed westward along the north channel to Weighton Lock or beyond, where deep water can be held right around the bight to Apex Light at Trent Falls. Care must be taken at this western end, however, to steer for the Apex Light and not to cut the corner at Faxfleet, for the mud here forms a considerable ness. Weighton Lock is conspicuous, being the only building feature on this whole shore. Entry is unrestricted by any bends or irregular nesses, but compensation for the vigorous tide must be made when approaching the lock on either flood or ebb. Moorings can be had in either the entrance to the lockpit, where boats will sit firmly on the level lock sill at LWS, or alternatively just outside the lockpit, where a short line of mooring posts on the eastern side offers a none to robust fixing point which allows a boat to bottom in soft, and gently sloping mud. A mast rope is a wise precaution for fin keeled craft, although the author has experienced no trouble with falling over.

FACILITIES

Water may be obtained from the lock keeper, but there are no more facilities close to hand. There are, however, extremely pleasant and dry walks of a mile and a half to either Faxfleet to the south west, or to Broomfleet to the north east, a delightful and remote village which contains a post office, a general store, a telephone and a useful if unprepossessing pub.

Weighton Lock

Brough

Home of the Humber Yawl Club since 1919, Brough is undoubtedly the best known and best used of the Humber havens. Its location, next to major road and rail communications with Hull and the West Riding, has encouraged its development, but it has no particular advantages as a haven over many others, and it stands as a significant pointer to the potential of many Humber havens should ever the demand be increased and the access improved. Until the opening of Hull Marina, Brough was almost synonymous with pleasure sailing on the Humber. This is now, of course, no longer so, but it remains the headquarters of a lively and friendly yacht club and for this reason is well worth a visit.

APPROACHES and ENTRY

The upper Humber, and particularly the section near Brough, is so changeable that it is of little value to make recommendations about approaches. The Humber Conservancy surveyors, now part of Associated British Ports, operate their survey vessel out of Brough haven, and a chart is produced every two months. An up to date ABP chart is a vital prerequisite for anyone sailing in this area.

The position of Brough haven can be easily identified, being immediately upstream of the large hangars of the British Aerospace aircraft factory and immediately downstream of Gresham's timber yard.

The approach is best made about one hundred metres upstream of the tide gauge and the principal nesses in the sinuous channel are marked by posts surmounted by green or red flags, to be left to the appropriate side. The highest mud spit is on the western hand and care must be taken, if approaching on a flood tide, not to be set on to this.

BROUGH

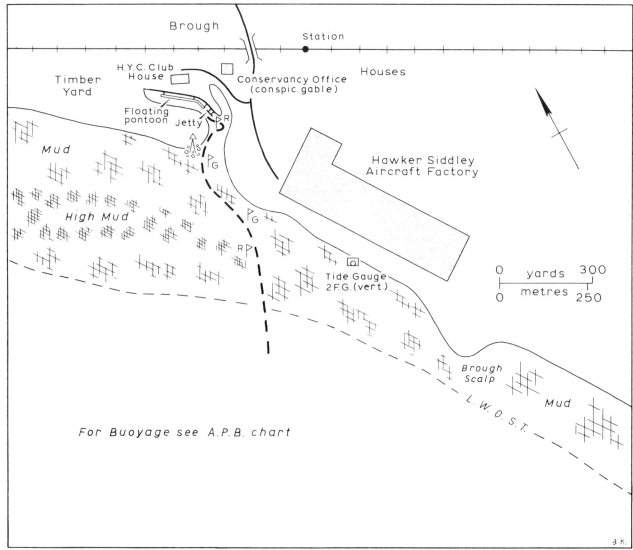

The haven entrance is fairly conspicuous, and a large beacon with a triangular topmark sits upon a stone bank on the port hand side. Entry is made midway between this beacon and the starboard marker post on the end of the spit opposite.

MOORINGS

Brough haven is owned by the Humber Yawl Club, and they have laid out, along the longer, western arm of the creek, an extensive floating pontoon to which boats moor either stern or bow to, with the other end made fast to sunken moorings. Extreme care must be taken when navigating Brough haven not to foul one's propeller or keel on the ubiquitous mooring ropes.

It is best for the visitor to make fast, in the first instance, to the large fixed jetty at the seaward end of the moorings, near to the Conservancy vessel. Club officials will then inform as to whether it is better to moor there or whether a suitable member's berth is available. In any event, the mud is of an extremely soft consistency in which boats float up to their marks.

FACILITIES

Brough offers excellent facilities. The Humber Yawl Club clubhouse is close at hand, and is always open at weekends and for longer periods in the summer. Here drinks, snacks, washing and clothes drying facilities are available to the visiting yachtsman. Farther afield, though not much farther, is the railway station, with frequent train services to Hull, Goole, Doncaster, London, Selby, Leeds, Manchester and York. Beyond lies the village of Brough, with shops, banks and two large pubs which serve meals and good beer.

Hessle

It is a pity that Hessle haven is so congested and industrialised, for it has the potential of being one of the most attractive of the Humber havens. Although caught up in Hull's suburban sprawl, Hessle village is in a delightful location where the wooded wolds sweep down to the Humber. Trees, cliffs, fine Victorian houses, green open spaces and foreshore walks rank among its visual pleasures and to these has been more recently added the breathtaking spectacle of the Humber bridge. Unfortunately, the haven has been crowded out by the encroachment of Dunston's shipyard. It is a shipyard of some note to sailormen, for it brought forth the *Winston Churchill*, but shipyards are shipyards and this particular one uses Hessle haven to fit out its products, with the result that the haven more often than not resembles a tiny sparrow's nest with a huge ungainly cuckoo flopping all over it.

APPROACHES,
ENTRY
and
MOORINGS

Hessle haven is conspicuous from the river, being located immediately upstream of the cranes and slipways of Dunston's shipyard. The sharp spire of Hessle church in the background provides an additional confirmatory feature. Entry can be made safely with a 5 feet draught boat two hours either side of high water springs, though a high water entry at neap tides is recommended for such a draught. The deepest water lies slightly to the east of centre in the haven entry, and a very high shingle bank lies on the port hand, fronting the clump of bushes and the broken fence. Once in the haven, the east side holds the

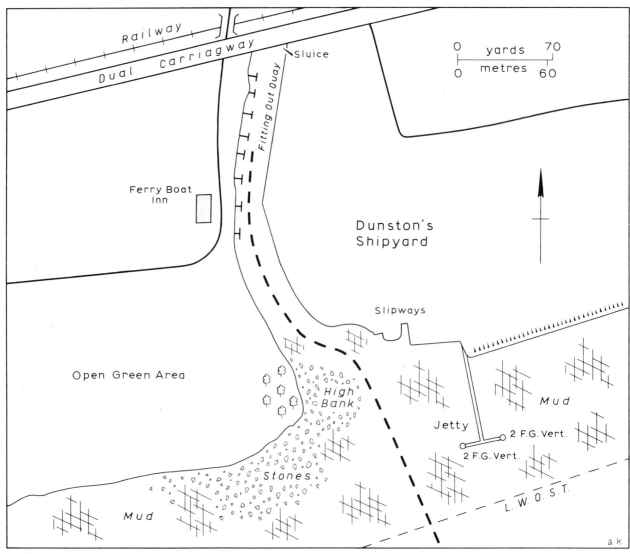

HESSLE

Hessle Haven and the bridge

deepest water right up to the sluice under the road and railway bridge, though the presence of a large Dunston's vessel may force the incoming skipper to keep nearer to the western bank.

Space in the haven is extremely limited, and the handful of jetties are usually occupied by the home-based boats. The visitor may be lucky enough to find a vacant one, but if not, a temporary mooring may be had outside another boat or on Dunston's quay itself where space permits. The fitting-out activities keep the mud soft, providing a comfortable low water lie.

FACILITIES

The large village of Hessle, with a variety of shops, pubs and restaurants, is situated only half a mile inland of the haven. Even nearer at hand, in a westerly direction is Hessle station, with a frequent train service to Hull, Goole, Selby and Leeds. Indeed, the thunder of trains across the sluice at the head of the haven is one of the least attractive features of an evening spent here. The Ferry Boat Inn, next to the moorings, is a large and popular pub; the landlord keeps a boat in the haven and he usually spares no effort to see that a visiting boat is safely accommodated. Dunston's yard, though an eyesore in some senses, is interesting in others, and can provide useful services at times should the metalwork of a visiting craft be in any way fatigued.

Hessle Haven and Dunston's shipyard

Hull

Hull is a fine city. Its fame stems from its recently relinquished position as Britain's premier deep sea fishing port, but its roots penetrate deep into medieval history and spread over centuries of commercial importance in the Baltic trade and the Greenland whale fishery. The blitz destroyed much of its old quarter, but lots more remains to be seen, and the city offers some architectural masterpieces spanning three centuries of civic dignity. As the undisputed capital of the cruising ground covered in this pilot it merits an extended visit from the cruising yachtsman.

APPROACHES
(See Admiralty chart no. 3497 or ABP chart *Spurn Head to Barton Haven*)

The perennial importance of Hull as a port stems from the fact that the deep water channel of the Humber sweeps around the bight from Paull to Hessle and keeps the roads clear of sand and silt. Approaches from up or down stream, therefore, present no problems at any stage of the tide. Shipping, either moving or at anchor, need be the only focus of concern.

The small boat skipper approaching from seaward on the second half of a flood tide, however, or conversely leaving Hull on the first of the ebb, can usually cut the Skitter corner and avoid a lengthy detour around the bight. The Hull middle sand dries out, but can easily be cleared by boats drawing 5 feet (1·5 metres) any time from half tide up. When to this knowledge is added the fact that the flood runs up in Hull Roads for three quarters of an hour after it has started to ebb away over the Skitter, the yachtsman is presented with a welcome variety of strategies in which he can play wind, tide and time against each other. Spring tides can attain five knots in Hull Roads, so great forethought must be exercised at all times to prevent being swept past one's destination.

ENTRY

The most conspicuous landmark on the waterfront of central Hull is the 'water gate' – a tidal surge barrier spanning the entrance to the river Hull. Upstream of this is the Victoria Pier, only a shadow of its former double-decked magnificence, but still a prominent and popular amenity backed by a tree-lined street. Upstream of this again is Minerva Pier which forms the downstream rim of Humber Dock Basin, the entrance to Hull's Marina. Entry into the basin is relatively hazard free, provided allowance is made for the vigorous sideways component given by the tidal stream.

MOORINGS

Humber Dock Basin, once the muddy home of Paull shrimpers and other assorted craft, is the tidal entrance to Hull Marina, an excellent yachting facility second to none on the east coast of England. The Marina (☎ 0482 25048, VHF Ch 80) is staffed 24 hours a day all year round. The lock operates three hours either side of high water, and throughout the penning period vessels drawing up to two metres can cross the sill. Deeper draughted vessels must pass in or out nearer high water, but once inside are guaranteed a minimum depth of 4·5m. Traffic signals operate on the western side of the entrance to Humber Dock Basin: two green lights over one white indicate that the lock is open to seaward; three red lights indicate that it is closed.

Minerva Pier with entrances to the Marina and Fish Dock beyond

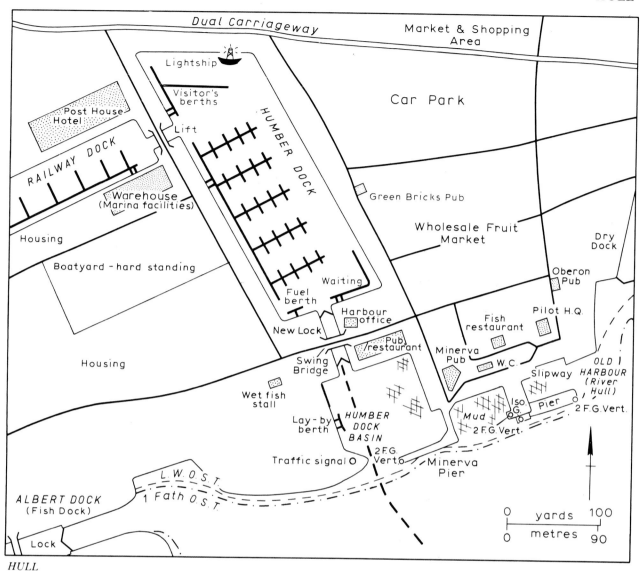

Dual Carriageway

Market & Shopping Area

Lightship

Visitor's berths

Lift

Post House Hotel

RAILWAY DOCK

HUMBER DOCK

Car Park

Warehouse (Marina facilities)

Housing

Boatyard - hard standing

Green Bricks Pub

Wholesale Fruit Market

Dry Dock

Oberon Pub

Fuel berth

Waiting

Pilot H.Q.

Fish restaurant

New Lock

Harbour office

Housing

Pub restaurant

Minerva Pub

W.C.

Slipway

OLD HARBOUR (River Hull)

Swing Bridge

Wet fish stall

Lay-by berth

HUMBER DOCK BASIN

Mud

2 F.G. Vert.

Iso. G.

Pier

2 F.G.Vert.

Traffic signal

2 F.G. Vert

Minerva Pier

L.W.O.S.T.

ALBERT DOCK (Fish Dock)

1 Fath O.S.T.

Lock

0   yards   100
0   metres   90

Entrance to Hull Marina at low water

Congestion in Hull's old harbour on the river Hull

There are 290 berths in the Marina and 20 are reserved for visiting yachts. Immediately to starboard on entering Humber Dock is a waiting berth and immediately to port are fuel, water and pump-out facilities. The 1991 rates for visiting yachts are £0.35 per foot per day, £1.60 per foot per week and £4.40 per foot per month.

Craft arriving in Humber Dock Basin outside penning times can reach either the lay by berth to port or the Minerva Pier berth to starboard at any state of the tide if drawing no more than 2 metres.

FACILITIES

It would be a pointless and impossible task to enumerate the facilities which Hull can offer to yachtsmen. Any kind of victual or service is available there. One particular advantage, and worthy of emphasis, is the central location of Humber Dock. All too often, in large ports, the small boat moorings are far removed from the city centre. In Hull, the bustling market, the financial district, the department stores and transport facilities are all at hand. The Marina itself offers chandlery, toilet, shower and bar services and there are excellent facilities for hoisting out and repair. Once again, craft can be seen in the very centre of Hull and the citizens can receive a constant reminder of the maritime traditions which made their city great.

Hedon Haven

In mediaeval times Hedon was a commercial centre and port of considerable significance. Indeed, in the twelfth century, it was a more important borough and harbour than Hull. Today, its church, the King of Holderness, alone testifies to this former glory. Progressive silting of the haven, the increase in size of commercial vessels and competition from nearby Hull spelled its doom as a port. Long before the final closure of the haven in 1971, commercial keels and lighters had ceased to use Hedon. Now, as so often is the case in these waters, the drainage authorities have erected a sluice, leaving a rump of a haven whose only connection with Hedon is in name.

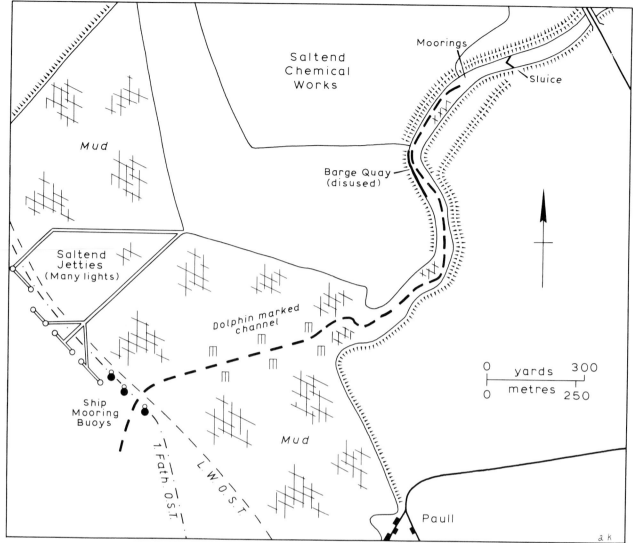

Moorings

Saltend
Chemical
Works

Sluice

Barge Quay
(disused)

Saltend
Jetties
(Many lights)

Mud

Dolphin marked
channel

Ship
Mooring
Buoys

Mud

0   yards   300
0   metres   250

1 Fath. O.S.T.

L.W.O.S.T.

Paull

HEDON HAVEN

Yet this stunted haven does continue to provide more moorings than any other place within easy striking distance of Hull. Add to this the fact that it is free, and its popularity with local fishermen is easily understood. It is difficult to imagine, however, why a visiting yachtsman would ever entertain the idea of entering Hedon Haven. Caught short of Hull on the flood and lacking power, a visitor would be better advised to cross the river to Skitter or North Killingholme; if a northerly or easterly wind made the Yorkshire bank more attractive, then nearby Paull offers an excellent offshore anchorage with many facilities in the village.

APPROACHES and ENTRY
(See Admiralty chart no. 3497, or ABP chart *Spurn Head to Barton Haven*)

Hedon Haven lies between the Saltend oil jetties and the old fishing village of Paull, both of which are extremely conspicuous features of the Humber waterfront in this area. Hard by the downstream end of the Saltend jetties are three black buoys, used for attaching the lines of large tankers lying at the jetty. Entry to the haven is best made by passing between any of these buoys, though if ship's lines obstruct, then pass as close to them as is feasible. From this point, the channel to the actual haven entry is remarkably straight and remarkably stable. Three pairs of substantial dolphins mark the channel, and vessels must pass between each pair in turn. The first port hand dolphin is deteriorated, and is less massive than the others, but all of them are very conspicuous, and even at the highest of spring tides, when the bulk of the woodwork is covered, a large baulk projects as a topmark from each one and is always clearly visible. The channel in the haven proper offers no navigational problems, for the deepest water is in the middle right up to the sluice. Craft drawing 5 feet (1·5m) may enter and leave the haven two hours either side of high water.

61

Hedon Haven – paradise lost?

Hedon's rump of a haven

MOORINGS

Numerous small boat mooring jetties, mainly belonging to local fishermen, have been constructed out from both banks for three hundred yards downstream from the sluice. Since most of the fishermen of Hedon Haven are part time small boat operators, the visiting yachtsman will be extremely fortunate to find any of these moorings vacant for more than the duration of one tide. Should he be lucky, however, he may allow his boat to settle with impunity, for the silt is beautifully soft, and the local boat will have dug out a flat platform to sit in.

Since the cessation of oil lighter activity at the BP quay in 1973, this provides the most certain opportunity for a temporary berth. The bottom used to be rather more hard and irregular than farther up the haven, and the covering of soft silt which has occurred since the barges withdrew ought not to lull the fin-keeled skipper into a sense of false security. A mast rope is a wise precaution at this quay.

FACILITIES   Hedon Haven offers nothing to the visitor. A rather muddy scramble along the haven banks leads ultimately to a two mile walk to either Paull or Hedon, both of which are well worth a visit, but which are more attractively reached from an anchorage off Paull than from Hedon Haven. Some havens can be recommended for their solitude, others for the rural walks they offer to the cruising man anxious to discover new places; Hedon Haven is dominated and destroyed in both these respects by the stinking, smouldering, humming chemical works that broods over it. If it ever was a paradise, it is now indisputably lost.

Stone Creek

During the eighteenth century, Sunk Island was connected to the north bank of the Humber in a massive reclamation project which resulted in the loss of one haven and the gain of another. Patrington Haven, of considerable earlier commercial importance, became separated from the Humber by several miles of reclaimed land. The construction of sea walls and sluices for protection and drainage meant that navigable water was withdrawn by stages from Patrington. The final stage in the process occurred in 1975, when a new sluice was built at the very mouth of the creek, removing the last vestige of a haven from the map.

STONE CREEK (APPROACHES)

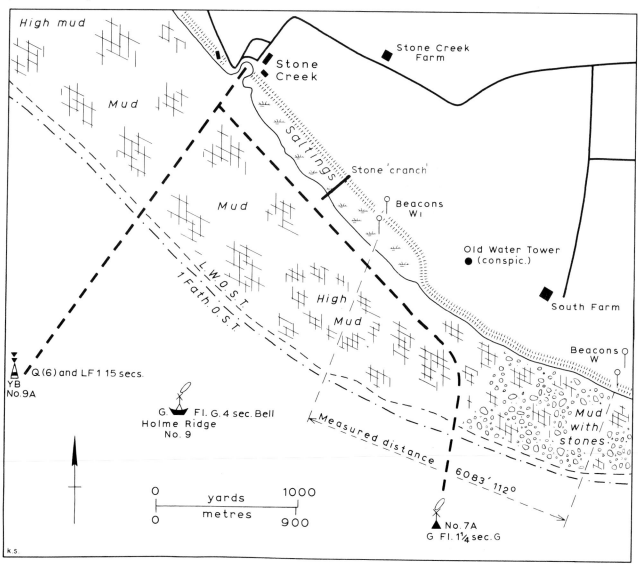

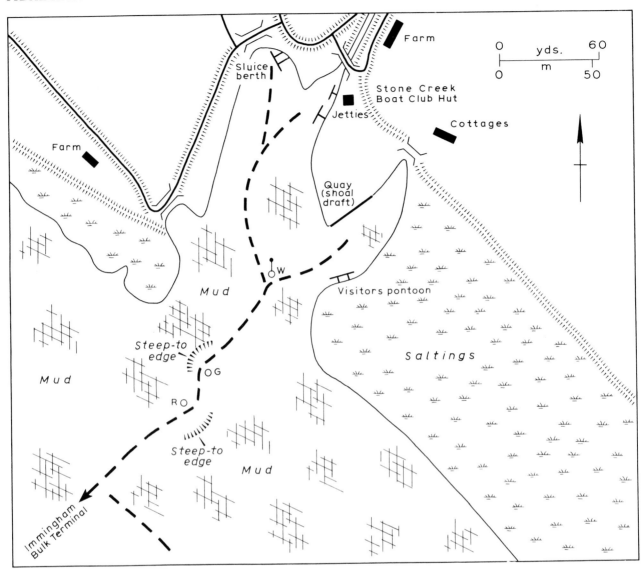

STONE CREEK (ENTRY)

The outfalls of the main Sunk Island drains at Stone Creek, however, have resulted in the creation of a new haven. In many respects, Stone Creek is a good haven, providing shelter and safety on a long and unbroken stretch of coast. Its remoteness, however, has ensured that it remains of importance only to local-based yachtsmen with private transport rather than to the visitor.

Stone Creek with Immingham across the Humber

APPROACHES   One hour each side of mean tides, the approaches to Stone Creek pose no problems. A direct passage over the sand from a point just upstream of 9A buoy can be made with 5 feet (1·5m) draught, and the only caution of note is to take care not to be swept by the tide either up or down stream more than a quarter of a mile, for the sand dries significantly higher in both these directions. On high spring tides, this approach can be used 1½ hours either side with safety, but on neap tides a boat drawing 5 feet (1·5m) is not advised to make it. A safe bearing for this direct approach is 045 degreesT, keeping the conspicuous Immingham bulk terminal astern.

Another approach to Stone Creek gives more tidal scope. Indeed, it offers a half tide passage to boatmen with local knowledge, but safe limits for visitors are two hours either side of a mean tide for 5 feet (1·5m). Given that the visitor will most likely be approaching Stone Creek on the flood and leaving on the ebb, the orientation of this approach is particularly useful. A line from the main channel buoy 7A to the old water tower will give the best depth that can be achieved by a straight course. When within 40 to 50 metres from the sea wall, turn and run parallel until the outer entry mark for Stone Creek is abeam.

ENTRY   The nesses of mud, so typical of Humber haven entrances, are present at Stone Creek and their precise position in the outer parts is subject to variation. The yacht club attempts to keep a standard system of red and green lateral buoyage to indicate the nesses, and a white buoy with topmark must be closely approached before turning into the east or west arms of the haven.

MOORINGS   The moorings in Stone Creek are all private and are usually occupied by the home-based boats, but the Stone Creek Boat Club members are very hospitable and have available for visitors an excellent floating pontoon in the position indicated in the sketch chart. In most parts of the haven the mud is soft and boats will settle almost to their marks. For larger vessels there is a good overnight berth in the western sluice, though the usual caveats about the hazards of sluicing must be added. With careful attention to fender boards, mast rope and off-pull lines this can indeed be a very satisfactory berth, though the visitor will have to rely on the good offices of the nearby cottagers to provide a ladder for low water access.

FACILITIES   There are houses at Stone Creek from which water is obtainable and which will no doubt supply rural produce as it is available. More substantial supplies and facilities, however, are not to hand. Two miles away, the land reclaimers optimistically laid out a village centre, with church, school and telephone, but farms were built in the middle of their land and the village never got off the ground. Now the church stands empty and the school is a private house, lonely testament to an early planning venture that failed. Only the phone still works.

The village of Ottringham is six and a half miles from Stone Creek – far enough to deter even the most intrepid investigator, but if the visitor is fortunate enough to have transport laid on from the landward side, then he will be able to find basic food, meat, beer and petrol in the village.

Tidal Streams

The Admiralty Tidal Stream Atlas *NP 252 North Sea, Southern Portion* is not only at too small a scale to be useful in this cruising ground, but it under reports the strengths of the streams in some instances to a dangerous extent. It has been thought advisable, therefore, to construct a tidal stream series for the area, based on the most appropriate and strategic tidal diamonds of all the local large scale Admiralty charts. The selection of a time datum presented a problem. Most atlases refer to H.W. Dover; most local tide tables, even as far afield as Wells and Blakeney, are based on Hull Fish Dock. It was decided to use the last, on the grounds that these times are those which the local cruising yachtsman is most likely to have in the pocket of his jeans. Moreover, Hull is a convenient round five hours before H.W. Dover, so it does not require Einsteinian mathematical skills to make the conversion.

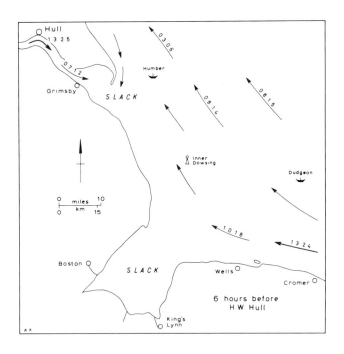

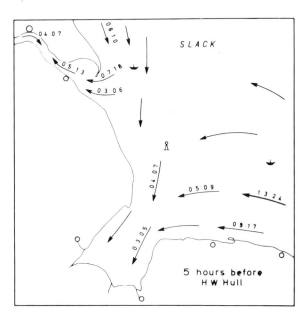

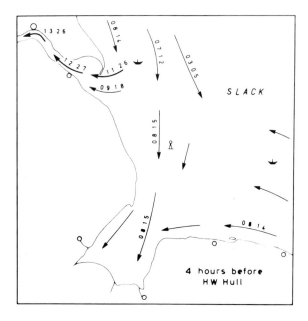

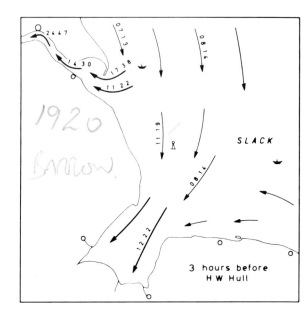

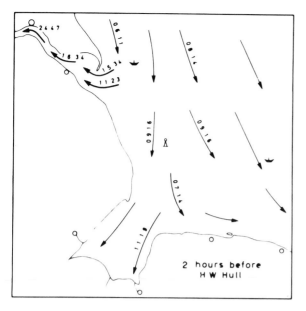

2 hours before
H W Hull

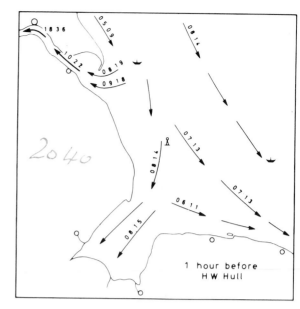

2040

1 hour before
H W Hull

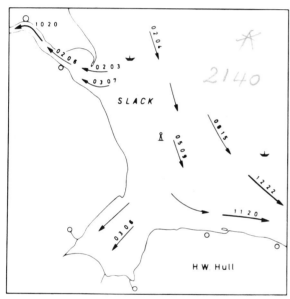

SLACK

2140

H.W. Hull

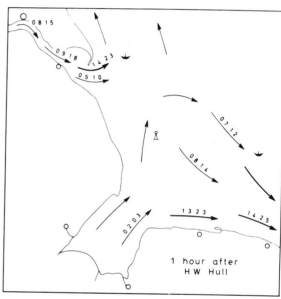

1 hour after
H.W. Hull

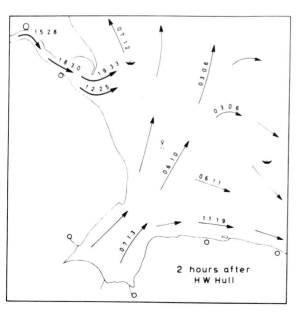

2 hours after
H.W. Hull

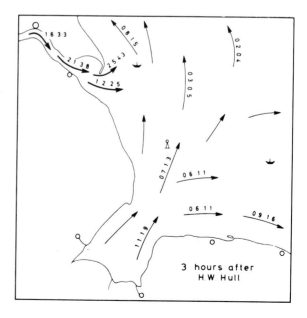

3 hours after
H.W Hull

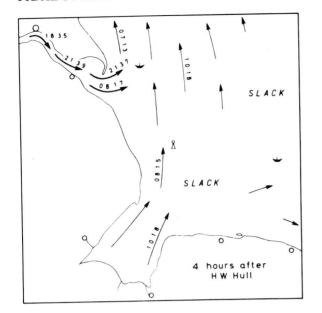

4 hours after
H W Hull

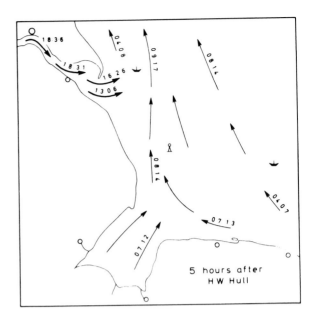

5 hours after
H W Hull

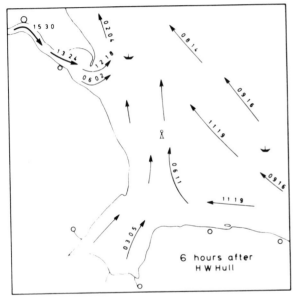

6 hours after
H W Hull

Distances and Tidal Information

	Distances from Hull Fish Dock (sea miles)	Tidal differences on Hull Fish Dock (add to or subtract from H.W. Hull)	Rise of tide at selected points	
			Springs	Neaps
Hull (Fish Dock)			22·3 feet (6·8m)	11·2 feet (3·4m)
New Holland	2·0			
Barrow	3·0	+ 8m(S) +15m(N)	23·0 feet (7·0m)	9·8 feet (3·0m)
Barton	4·5			
Hessle	3·7			
Ferriby Sluice	7·6	+12m(S) +25m(N)	22·0 feet (6·7m)	9·8 feet (3·0m)
Brough (via Read's I.)	11·5	+19m(S) +34m(N)	22·0 feet (6·7m	11·2 feet (3·4m)
Trent Falls	15·0	+30m(S) +50m(N)	18·1 feet (5·5m)	10·5 feet (3·2m)
Goole	24·0	+1hr.5m(S) +1h.20m(N)	18·1 feet (5·5m)	8·9 feet (2·7m)
Keadby	24·5	+1hr(S) +1hr.25m(N)	14·8 feet (4·5m)	9·2 feet (2·8m)
Hedon Haven	3·8	−10m	21·7 feet (6·6m)	10·8 feet (3·3m)
N. Killingholme	6·8	−23m(S) −18m(N)	21·0 feet (6·4m)	10·5 feet (3·2m)
Grimsby (via Burcom Flats)	14·0	−40m(S) −30m(N)	19·7 feet (6·0m)	9·8 feet (3·0m)
Haile Sand Fort (Tetney)	19·0	−50m	19·0 feet (5·8m)	9·2 feet (2·8m)
Haile Sand Buoy	24·0	−1hr		
Saltfleet	31·0	−50m		
Wainfleet	54·0	Same		
Boston (via Wainfleet)	72·0	+11m	22·0 feet (6·7m)	9·8 feet (3·0m)
Fosdyke (via Wainfleet)	73·0	+15m		
Sutton Bridge	74·0	+ 8m		
Wisbech	81·5	+18m		
Dog-in-a-Doublet Sluice	95·6	+1h.43m		
Lynn	74·0	+15m	22·3 feet (6·8m)	9·8 feet (3·0m)
Denver Sluice	88·0	+1hr.15m	9·8 feet (3·0m)	5·6 feet (1·7m)
Burnham Flats Buoy	51·6	− 8m	19·7 feet (6·0m)	9·2 feet (2·8m)
Brancaster Bar	62·1	Same	19·0 feet (5·8m)	10·2 feet (3·1m)
Burnham Harbour Mouth	62·6	Same	18·1 feet (5·5m)	9·8 feet (3·0m)
Wells Fairway Buoy	63·4	Same	17·4 feet (5·3m)	9·5 feet (2·9m)
Wells Quay	65·5	+35m		
Blakeney Wreck Buoy	67·5	+ 8m	16·4 feet (5·0m)	8·5 feet (2·6m)
Blakeney Pit	69·5	+30m		

Index